P

Finding the Pearl is a call to action. Too often we buy into the mindset that others will take care of us whether we can accept more responsibility or not. This true story is for everyone and every age from 9 to 99. It can be read again and again when you encounter the challenges of your very existence. You will find yourself thinking and believing that you, too, are capable of great works and great influence. Read along—no, experience along—with Thuan the wonders of her life.

Chris Hilicki
Founder Dalmatian Press Children's Books

Nothing is as inspiring and motivational as living Tammy's journey through this book. *Finding the Pearl* paints a vivid picture of her struggles and determination to become the wonderful person she is today. Her story reminds me of the saying, "If you think you can't or you think you can, you will be right."

Dr. Larry Ohlhauser, M.D.
The Healthy CEO

In this truly inspiring story, Tammy uses her can-do attitude to move from victim to victor as she overcomes insurmountable obstacles. I strongly recommend this quick-paced read to everybody who wants to realize a better life. As an "outsider" who risked my life for the blessed opportunities of the American Dream, I salute Tammy for sharing her story of a job well done!

Jin Kyu (Suh) Robertson, Ph.D.
Author of *Major Dream: From Immigrant Housemaid to Harvard Ph.D.*

Although at times it is gut-wrenching to witness her pain, I was drawn to Thuan's (Tammy Fadler's) independent nature throughout *Finding the Pearl.* This book takes readers into the stench of the market, the chilling aspects of war, the horror of Tet. Yet she finds the courage and hope to rise above it all. Thuan's willingness to make the best of her circumstances—is her redemption.

Dr. Michelle Robin
Author of *Wellness on a Shoestring*

Little did I realize when I first met Tammy Fadler what a wonderful journey it would be.

I'd never met a person who started with so little in material blessings, yet managed to accomplish so much. Arriving in America "vertically challenged" with only broken English and ten dollars to her name, this little lady set her jaw and faced her challenges squarely.

A firm belief that failure is not an option is her daily mantra and stands her in good stead. Understanding her immigrant background and lack of formal education, I once asked, "Tammy, how do you handle discrimination?" She replied simply, "What's that?"

Tammy makes it nearly impossible to discriminate against her. She will ignore you, go around you or go over you—and you will love her in the process. Not that she hasn't dealt with failure and disappointment. But, to her, setbacks are mere opportunities for lessons gleaned along the way.

This petite fireball rapidly rose from real estate rookie to land in the top one-tenth of the million-plus realtors in the United States. She travels the world over while maintaining her spiritual and physical life. Amazing.

This is Tammy's story. An edgy story from the real world. A story rich with spunk, determination and a can-do attitude. This is her life, these are her experiences.

Dr. Thomas Hill
Eagle Goal Coach, Inc.
Eagle Summit Cofounder

Finding the Pearl

2013
Eric Hoffer Award
FINALIST

EDITOR & PUBLISHER
EPPY Awards
Autobiography/Memoir

SAN FRANCISCO
book festival

Finding the Pearl

Thuan Tammy Fadler

with Carol McAdoo Rehme

Finding the Pearl:
Unstoppable passion, unbridled success

By Thuan Tammy Fadler with Carol McAdoo Rehme

Published by:
Publishing Directions, LLC
P. O. Box 715
Avon, CT 06001-0715

ISBN: 978-1-928782-30-8
LCCN: 2011918166

Cover Designed by 1106 Design

Printed in the United States

This book is dedicated to
Huỳnh Văn Bé (Dad) and Trần Thị Hòa (Mom)
to honor their enduring love of family.

Table of Contents

If it's to be, it's up to me.

Introduction

It is dark in the cabin of China Southern flight #0328, bound for Guangzhou. The tiny reading light makes my tears barely noticeable to the passengers sleeping around me. Upon reading Tammy Fadler's biography *Finding the Pearl,* my spirit is alive with possibility and potential. My heart is full of joy, my mind is racing with ideas and my soul is celebrating with hope and awe!

With each turn of the page, I was riveted by Tammy's drive, determination and positive outlook to overcome horrific circumstances. Her raw resolution is evident in accounts of her early childhood in war-torn Vietnam, and her spirit continues undaunted as she navigates a huge swath of work experiences, relationships, cultural differences and other roadblocks.

When I relate Tammy's journey to my own, I am inspired by her strength and fortitude. As a single mother in the 1980s, I—like Tammy—saw entrepreneurship as the only way to achieve the life I wanted for myself and my three sons; I, too, chose real estate to help meet those goals. Knowing firsthand the difficulties of starting from scratch while trying to support a family, I simply cannot imagine layering the additional challenge of doing it in an unfamiliar country.

This book is full of gritty lessons drawn from a child's focused and unwavering dreams in the streets of Saigon. Tammy's resilience and plucky ability to pick herself up and move forward are admirable. From the streets of Khanh Hoi, where she peddled fish to provide for her family, to the days when she was featured in national publications, her style and technique forged success.

Anyone—entrepreneurs, businesspeople, those struggling to find a way through life—can find inspiration and wisdom in her story. The fundamental principles she models apply to any person, any business, any goal; they benefit and motivate us all. Tammy demonstrates with great examples, and great passion, how to overcome the obstacles that appear in our lives so that we, too, are unstoppable in our quest for success. Her book is heartfelt, honest, reliable—and life changing.

Cordia Harrington, CEO
The "Bun Lady"
Tennessee Bun Company

Foreword

You have something special, you have greatness within you. Tammy Fadler, she calls that "Finding the Pearl" when you discover your greatness. When you discover the work you are supposed to do. Tammy believes there is a calling in your life and everything that you experience, brings you to where you are right now.

She has gone through a lot, she has seen a lot. She has empowered and inspired her family. She came here as an immigrant and as an entrepreneur she already made her mark. She encourages you to find the pearl. It has been said that the two most important moments in our lives, the day that we are born and the day we realize why we were born. That day, when we find that pearl. That day, when we find what is in our heart.

This book will not only introduce you to her experiences and what she has gone through but they will provide in this book methods and techniques and strategies that will teach you how to find your pearl. How to overcome the challenges of life and make it through the storms of life.

Finding the Pearl changed my life and my family's life and it will change your life. When you put the pages down, when you go through the chapters, I guarantee you; you will never be the same again. Finding the Pearl is a book whose time has come and will change millions of lives. That's my story and I'm sticking to it.

Les Brown
World's Leading Motivator

CHAPTER 1

Government School, circa 1958
Khánh Hội, Việt Nam

Girl with Answers

"Good morning, children."

The students rose in unison. Crossing their arms and bowing in respect, they greeted the teacher. "*Chào*, Thầy."

Chairs scraped and grins erupted as the eight-year-olds jostled each other to resume their seats at the crowded tables.

I could reach out and touch him. Thuận nodded in satisfaction at the thought, yet ducked her head to hide her heated cheeks. Tugging the edge of her tunic, faded and stained, she peeked from the corner of her eyes at her beloved teacher's face as the classroom settled into order. At home, her family teased her for being First-Table Student, but Thuận didn't mind. Her seat at the front got her nearer Ông Thầy; she never missed a word spoken from his mouth. And it was but a quick step to the chalkboard when he called on her to solve a multiplication problem.

Those solutions came easily to Thuận. The same was true of many other students as well, in part because Thuận slipped them the answers. And her answers were correct. Most of the time. Thuận cast a calculating look at Phượng, wondering what food her classmate might offer today in exchange for the final solutions to their mathematics quiz. Rice? Mangosteen?

Thuận shifted in her chair, restless and pensive on this final day of class. *Four months.* She winced. A long time to wait for school to start again. She leaned forward to listen as her teacher addressed the students.

"You are hard working and bright. It was my good fortune to teach you all." His eyes, coffee bean brown, seemed to bore into hers alone. "This summer, I will offer lessons to prepare you for next school year."

Tutoring! Thuận's heart thumped against her chest and her thoughts raced at this unexpected opportunity. More lessons. More challenges. More problems to solve. More to learn at the feet of her wise teacher. More to . . . She nearly missed his next comment.

"For those whose families can pay a fee, come to my home the day of . . ."

A fee? Thuận knew her parents could not pay. Even with Má's fish stall in the marketplace and Ba's day labor at the shipyard, it was a daily struggle to provide rice and fish sauce for dinner for so many hungry bellies at home. She swallowed hard against her disappointment and struggled to keep her attention on the morning's lessons.

As she slouched out of the cinderblock compound in late morning, Thuận shielded her eyes against the stinging glint of sunlight from the school's tin roof.

Phượng, in her crisp new pants, sauntered close, surrounded by a gaggle of girls. "It is agreed? We all go for lessons with Ông Thầy?" The girls giggled and nodded, not even noticing how Thuận slowed her steps until she lagged far behind them. Thuận gazed back at the courtyard flagpole and chewed her lower lip.

"First-Table Student," she reminded herself out loud. The girl overflowing with so many answers she gave them to others. She squared her shoulders and resolved to find a way to attend the tutoring session with the others.

Determined to earn the fee on her own, Thuận capitalized on the only commodity she had for sale—her willingness to work. She balled her hand into a fist then flexed it open wide at the idea. She knew she was as thin as a spoke on the bicycles crowding the streets of Sài Gòn; but, like Ba, she had a strong back and willing arms. With sure determination, Thuận scurried from house to house with offers for the lowliest of jobs.

"Pigs hungry? I feed pigs."

"Pens dirty? I clean pens."

"Need water? I bring water."

Those who had more *dong* than hours in their day were eager to employ her. Armed with empty buckets, she strode the dirt road to the district square and took her place behind a woman who was hunched from work into a human sickle. As the long line inched forward, Thuận tried to ignore the sweltering summer sun. She envied the government soldiers lounging across the street in the shade of a building. One sat on a bench in the cool, bouncing a laughing street orphan on his boot.

When it was her turn at last, Thuận placed a five-gallon tin bucket under a spigot on the concrete post while women on the other three sides chattered over her head. Holding her hand under the faucet, she cupped her palm for a quick, cooling drink. As soon as the bucket filled, Thuận lugged it aside, flinching when it grated against the cement plinth, and smoothly replaced it with another.

She slid a bamboo pole under the rope handles and grunted to heave the load over one shoulder. With a full bucket bowing the limber bamboo behind her and a second bucket swinging in front, she shuffled along, careful not to slosh.

Thuận lost count of the trips it took to fill each neighbor's water barrel throughout the summer. Her shoulders throbbed under the weight; the soggy cotton shirt plastered her back; clumps of long black hair stuck to her neck. With each trek, she calculated *dong*.

Carrying water, she decided, was not so bad. But, oh, the pigs. "Hungh," she snorted under her breath, then giggled at her near-perfect imitation of the rooting grunts of the swine she'd come to dislike so much.

"Hoink! Hoink!" their porcine squeals welcomed when she brought them scraps. One, sometimes two to a small pen, the wallowing porkers pressed against the slats, begging street urchins restless with hunger.

Thuận took a deep breath, holding it while she scraped and shoveled and scooped their waste into a dented bucket. Feverish with exertion, she expelled air in jerky seeps, trying to make her breath last until, desperate to fill her lungs again, she dared a reluctant gasp. Her chest burned with the stench, fecal and foul, that surrounded her. Strong ammonia stung her eyes. Her stomach heaved in rebellion at the sour singe of her throat.

No good to snivel, she told herself. *Just do.*

She poured the vile offal into the stream bordering her neighborhood, rinsed the bucket and scurried to scoop again.

"Hooo-ink! Hoo-ink!" She squealed back at the hogs. At every clean pen, she calculated more *dong*. Each load, each heavy step brought her closer to her dream of summer schooling.

After tedious weeks of hauling water, slopping pigs and mucking sties, Thuận squatted in the space she claimed as hers, a scant corner of the crowded bedroom shared with a brood of brothers and sisters. Reaching over the roll of her straw sleeping mat, she lifted her small pillow and pulled out the brown paper sack hidden there. With quick fingers, she unfolded the crisp crease at the top to admire the tidy stack inside, evidence of satisfied customers.

Adding the last few *dong* from the day's work, Thuận counted the paper bills she had hoarded with so much hope. Her eyes widened. She counted a second time. And a third. Enough for lessons with Ông Thầy!

The next morning, freshly scrubbed and rosy, Thuận waited at the stop for the rust-pocked bus, eager to rejoin her teacher and classmates. A shank of ebony hair swung across her shoulders as she bounced up the steps and edged onto a marred bench to sit, back straight and legs crossed primly at the ankles. One hand gripped a brown paper sack brimming with *dong* and bright expectation.

At the door of her teacher's house, she took a deep breath and knocked in rhythm to the rapid pounding in her chest.

"Welcome, Thuận." He was just as she remembered him. Tall, handsome, deep voiced.

She bowed with a greeting of her own, slipped her feet from her sandals and walked inside, waiting for her eyes to adjust after the brightness of the summer sun. She held out the brown bag with a hint of bashful pride. "My *dong*."

His forehead wrinkled in confusion. "*Dong*?"

"For tutoring, Thầy."

"Tutoring? But—it's too late."

"Too . . . late?" Her eyes widened; her thumping heart screeched to a halt.

"Summer is over, Thuận. The session is finished."

Over? Finished? She shook her head, trying to clear it. "But, but how . . ."

His voice, as gentle as his brown eyes, softened. Thickened. "I'm sorry you missed our classes. The students studied hard and did well."

Understanding pricked. Then, the thrust of full comprehension pierced her. So busy with the sweat of hard labor, so preoccupied with earning money for the fee, she had lost track of time. Summer slipped by, unnoticed. While she had slaved at the sties, her friends had sipped from the fountain of knowledge. Thuận nearly doubled over from the pain of her loss.

"Too bad, Thuận. I can see you are disappointed." He patted her drooping head. "Perhaps next summer?"

Next summer!

It was a long walk to the bus stop. The ride home was even longer. She stared sightlessly out the cracked window while fat tears plopped onto the brown sack crumpled in her lap. Silent sobs wracked her weary body as she tried to make sense of her summer.

With a final shuddery hiccup, Thuận swiped at her runny nose and leaned her forehead against the cool glass pane and moaned. Wasn't she First-Table Student? Girl with answers?

"But what good to have answers," she whispered to her watery reflection, "and never hear the questions?"

CHAPTER 2

Marketplace, circa 1959
Khánh Hội, Việt Nam

Buy My Fish

Rubber flip-flops slapped a puff of dust against her heels with every hurried step while the pointed tip of her tongue traced the edges of her lips to wet them. Once. Twice. She shrugged. Thirst would be easy to quench later with a stop at the district well. But the grumble in her belly was another matter entirely. Thuận slid both hands into the front pockets of her flour sack tunic and against her bony ribs she cradled them—two small bananas—as she hopped across deep ruts in the road.

Má will wonder what took me so long, she thought, and quickened her pace until she was almost running. School had ended promptly at 11 a.m. and Thuận knew she shouldn't loiter. She scooted out of the way of an armored military tank lumbering past and coughed at the clouds of dust it kicked into her face.

Her nose twitched. She smelled the marketplace even before she heard it. Rotted fruit fermenting in the hot sun. Vegetables wilted and decayed. And the stink of fish. Always the sharp stink of fish.

Thuận averted her eyes when she rounded the corner where squealing pigs had been slaughtered, holding her breath against the metallic scent of pooled blood. She scurried into the heart of the open marketplace. Leggy chickens squawked and scattered at her feet while she dodged an elbow, kicked at a gaunt dog and stepped over a pile of fresh dung.

Thuận saw Má squatted on the rented dirt-packed plot between twin tubs filled with flopping fish purchased early that morning from the fishmonger at the docks. Her conical hat shaded only her face.

"You like this one?" Má held out the black flathead to a customer. Giving a quick shake of his head, he turned away and was swept into the crowd. The fish would breathe a while longer. Má heaved a deep sigh of regret and slipped it back into the water.

"For dinner, Má." Thuận pulled the nearly-ripe bananas from her deep pockets.

"From Phượng?" Má's eyes, as warm as fish sauce, searched hers.

Thuận shrugged. It was a small thing to slip Phượng the mathematics answers that came more easily to her than her friend; Phượng was expected to do well in grade four. In return for the favor, she was always generous—fragrant bananas or sometimes scoops of rice from the full buckets at her parents' house. It was a smart partnership. Thuận had something Phượng wanted; Phượng had something Thuận wanted.

Má's fingers combed the length of her daughter's straight black hair, shiny warm from the blistering sun. She refastened the barrette that held it back from the neat part near Thuận's forehead. "Hurry now, *con*—my child. There are fish to sell before we eat."

Thuận nodded, understanding even at age ten, what she really meant: "A sale today means dinner tonight." The younger children depended on Thuận. Now it was time to set aside thoughts of school and get to work.

The round-nosed fish Má chose was thick and scaly. "Remember, twelve *dong*, Thuận. Nothing less." Her tone left no room for doubt. Thuận knew it was important to make enough profit to pay for today's stall and tomorrow's supply. If Fortune smiled, they might even have a fish for their own pot that night. Her mouth watered at the hopeful thought.

With a bowl held tight in the crook of her wiry arm, Thuận shoved her way into the jostling throng.

"A fine fat fish," she hawked. "Only twenty-five *dong*." Up and down the street she wove between vendors who quibbled with shoppers over withered vegetables and bruised fruit. She looked into each face, trying to catch an eye, hoping for a glimmer of interest.

"You buy my fish?" She pointed at her bowl. "My sister, she's sick."

Someone pushed; Thuận pushed back. Water sloshed and splashed into the vee neck of her shirt. She spread her fingers wide over the top of the bowl and hugged it against her thin chest to keep the fish from jumping out. A live fish, she'd learned, is always worth more than a dead fish.

"Eggs!" someone yelled.

"Watercress!" called another.

Realizing she had forgotten to get a drink, Thuận licked her parched lips and tried to ignore the persistent rumble in her stomach.

"Mint! Bamboo heart!"

"Peppers, spicy hot!" Their shouts, as sharp as sniper shots, filled the village streets.

Everyone in Khánh Hội, it seemed, had something to sell. Herbs they gleaned from the side of the road leading to Sài Gòn. Greens they harvested by standing knee-deep in the swamps, tossing and heaping fragrant stems high into baskets. Anything they could barter, trade or vend to feed their large families. It was a daily fight for survival and the marketplace was their battleground.

The stench of human sweat threatened to gag her. Thuận looked up, shouldering her way between the sardined bodies to search for a hint of sky or a breath—a single whiff—of sweet air. Sweat beaded her brow and she swallowed hard against the rancid burning in her throat.

"See my fish!" a young boy suddenly shouted nearby. Too near. "Only eighteen *dong*."

Thuận jerked around. Eighteen? Abruptly, she darted through the throng to position herself a short distance away. "My brother, he needs clothes," she hollered. It wasn't really a lie, she decided. They all needed clothes. "Buy *my* fish." Her shrill voice edged higher.

Thuận approached a tall, thin woman and shoved the bowl under her nose. "You see? Fresh today. For you, fifteen *dong*," she wheedled. "You want?"

"Ten." The counter offer was as clipped as an officer's orders.

"Twelve," Thuận insisted, relieved when the woman nodded her agreement and held out a wad of *dong*. Thuận slipped the money into the deep pocket of the loose, straight-legged pants Má had accepted from the American Red Cross and cut down to fit her oldest child. With a brisk nod, she flicked her wrist, inviting the woman to follow her. "Come. Má will clean the fish."

Thuận wove her way back to the stall, the customer at her heels.

"Money, Má." She cocked a brow. "Twelve *dong*."

When Má's mouth tightened as though she'd taken a wound to the belly, Thuận realized her mother had secretly hoped for more. After a slow nod, Má lifted the ebony fish from the bowl and whacked its head against a thick board. Thuận barely winced at the sound. With practiced skill and a sharp knife, Má quickly scaled and gutted the fish before handing it back to the customer.

Thuận peered into the galvanized tub, selecting a heavy flathead for her bowl. If she found a good customer, maybe Má could purchase wilted *raumuong*—wild spinach—at market's close. Added to flavor their usual pot of watery rice soup . . . She smacked her lips at the thought.

Thuận stiffened her spine, pushing aside thoughts of food. A scrawny chicken flapped its wings in half flight when she pushed purposefully back into the crowd, determined to sell another fish, to make just one more sale. She took a deep breath.

"A fine fat fish!" she shouted, loud enough to drown out the growling in her belly. "Only twenty-five *dong*."

CHAPTER 3

Testing Center, circa 1961
Khánh Hội, Việt Nam

Dragon Tails

Thuận shuddered as she stepped out of the harsh sunlight and into the testing center in Sài Gòn. She wrapped pencil-thin arms around herself against the sudden chill and blinked in the dimness. As she rounded the corner of the hallway, butterfly wings flittered inside her middle, reminding her of the feathered fans of a *Chàm* dance.

Weaving through the mass of clustered students, Thuận rose to her toes and extended her neck for a better view of the sheaf of papers posted on the wall. A frown knotted her forehead as she scanned the printed words.

Bính pointed to the list. "My name, it's there! Right there, see?" She hopped up and down in her excitement. "I did it. I did it!"

Thuận congratulated her classmate. "And mine? Do you see mine?" She turned to search the list again, eager to prove her own worth.

In spite of her nervous excitement, Thuận was certain she'd passed the extensive examinations. Wasn't that why she had always worked so hard in government school? To realize this single goal? For weeks she had waited impatiently to learn the final results, results that would separate the chaff from the rice. Like so many other eager students in Grade Five, she hoped to prove that the knowledge she had accumulated qualified her to continue on to the next level of education. If Fortune blessed her, a scholarship would be hers for the taking.

"Look. Over there." Phượng nudged her with a pointed little elbow. "I found my name."

Of course you did, thought Thuận and arched one eyebrow. *Most certainly because of the answers I traded to you in nearly every subject!* She forced herself to smile and nod at Phượng. No matter the outcome, their business arrangement had served them both well.

"My parents will be so pleased!" Her classmate melted into the throng of students who surged forward to learn their own results.

Singly and by groups, children left the building, some with beams as broad as the moon while others shuffled out in closed-face defeat.

Thuận's heartbeat quickened as she traced her hand along the long list of names. "Here I am, right here. Huỳnh Thị Thuận." She tapped a fingertip on the paper. "*My* name." She spun around with a smug grin. "You see?"

"We will go together." Bính's dark saucer eyes sparkled. She linked her elbow with her friend's. "Just think, Thuận. All the way through the next level, the two of us will be together—grades six through nine."

The girls flew on winged feet to the bus stop. On the ride back to Khánh Hội, Bính chattered excitedly, but Thuận gave dreamy nods of careless assent, responding only when she felt pressed. She gazed out the window into the buttery sunlight while fantasies of school swirled through her head like the fairytale dragons at a *Tết* celebration. She tried to grab hold of one colorful tail and follow it to the end, only to loosen her grasp and snag another vision when it drifted by.

Thuận couldn't remember *not* wanting to go to school. The lessons. The classwork. The assignments. She soaked up knowledge like a dried fish in soup. There was a deep yearning in her, a restless desire for something better. Something—more. More than a fish stall or a marketplace of vendors squatting on their rented square of dirt, haggling over baskets of figs and lemongrass. And education, she knew, was the key to the gate of her success.

Thuận wanted to be successful. She wanted a career—not a job. A career like those Ba spoke of with envy and longing in his voice.

All I really want is a chance, she thought, *a chance to be who I know I can become. And this is it, my opportunity.*

The future blossomed before her, a lotus unfurling its petals, and she was in the center of it all—floating in a graceful white *Áo dài,* the coveted uniform of the Second-Level school girls. Lác would be pleased for her, she knew. He shared her vision for a better life and, as best friends, they often shared this yearning for more schooling, their fondest dream.

Her parents would be so proud of their eldest child. She could hardly wait to tell them her happy news.

Thuận raced into the house.

"I did it!" Her tongue nearly tripped over the words as she threw herself into her father's arms. "I can go, Ba, I can go!" She squeezed him before turning to reach for Má.

"Go? Go Where? What is all this?" Má gripped Thuận's tapered shoulders and held her at arm's length.

"The examinations, Má, remember? I passed! So did Bính. And Phượng, as well. So many of my other friends, too, found their names on the list. All of us will go to Second Level!"

Ba closed his eyes with a slight shake of his head. Má's mouth thinned. "No, Thuận, no more school."

"What? But . . . why?" A wave of heat swept over her and a lump the size of a coconut filled her throat.

"We cannot pay."

"But, I received top ranking and received the scholarship. Second Level will cost nothing." Expectantly, she turned to her father. "Ba?"

Her parents exchanged a long look. Ba shifted uneasily, wiped work-stained palms down the front of his thin black pants, and lowered his gaze.

Thuận's anguished protest broke the stretch of silence in the small room. "No money is needed! Don't you understand? The scholarship pays."

Má rolled her tired wrists. She stretched her fingers. With a long-suffering sigh, she looked her daughter squarely in the eye. "Scholarships pay for tuition, it is true. But it still takes money. Money for books. Money for supplies. Money for uniforms."

"Money we do not have," Ba pointed out, pursing his lips until the blood drained from them.

Má's voice gentled. "You cannot go, my child. For you, school is at an end."

"No!" With a cry as brittle as rice paper, Thuận crumpled to the floor in anguish. She folded her knees against her chest and buried her pale face into them.

Can't they see I deserve this? I studied hard. I passed the examination. They can't take this away from me. She clenched her arms around her legs, making herself as small as possible. *I earned the scholarship. It's mine, all mine! Don't they understand?*

She could almost see the dragon's gaping mouth as it turned to bite the fingers gripping the end of its tail. In the deepest corner of her mind, she knew her mother was right. The need at home was great. But . . . her heart yearned to hold on to the tail of her dreams a little bit longer.

Ba's hand, rough and calloused from his labor at the shipyard, brushed back the long sweep of hair that curtained her damp cheeks. "Accept it, *con*, it is your fate. No more school."

Thuận flinched at the finality of his words. She blinked several times to rid herself of the deep stinging behind her eyes and slowly raised her head. But she refused to meet their gazes. Instead, she stared into the far corner of the room.

"You are eldest," Má reminded. Her voice flattened. "It is time to work. Your brothers, your sisters, they must be fed. You will take a paying job."

Thuận stiffened. "But the fish stall . . ."

"You can help me there when you are not busy sewing for . . ."

"Sewing!"

". . . sewing for Dì Ba—Aunt Three."

"But . . ."

"You will start by cleaning the floors of her shop." Má's mouth thinned in a stern line. "Then, you learn to sew. It is a skill, a skill to bring sure, steady money to this household."

Má hesitated. She reached out a tentative hand and let it settle on her daughter's back for a long moment. "Thuận, you must understand. We simply do what we need to do."

Thuận's shoulders drooped. *Sewing instead of school? Stuck inside Dì Ba's small shop for long hours? Working all day—every day—while my friends study for a real career?*

Realization dawned. Money was no problem for Phượng's family. Even without any more of Thuận's answers, she would step into a bright future. *A future that belongs to me!*

It was a bitter melon to swallow.

Thuận's lips quivered in spite of herself. Stabbed by Fate's sudden fickleness, she fought the tears that threatened. Rising from the floor, she planted her feet and looked at Ba with pleading eyes, but he raised open palms and gave a glum shrug.

Defeated, she narrowed her gaze to Má's stony face, pursing her mouth as stubbornly as her mother's. *I* will *get an education. Someday, I will!* Following the rumble of the dragon, she clenched her fists and strode purposefully from the house.

CHAPTER 4

Embroidery Shop, circa 1965
Sài Gòn, Việt Nam

A Canvas Stretched

Thuận looked across the wooden embroidery frame to judge the work of her new sewing companion. *Thư's bouquet of pink orchids leans like a sleepy head,* she mused. *And that bird!*

Thuận nudged Thư's foot. "Do you need help? The bird wings are . . . they need a little . . . Here, let me see what I can do to help you."

The fourteen-year-olds exchanged places. With a few precise stitches, Thuận filled in the loose gaps to cover up rough edges. She selected some strands of bamboo green and with sparse, adept whips of her needle, added extra leaves to balance the tilting orchids.

"There."

Thư examined the stitching and nodded. Her cheeks, as round as tangerines, dimpled in gratitude. Thuận returned to her own station at the frame and decided to embroider a matching hornbill on her half of the intricate pattern.

This hooked beak looks just like Aunt Three's nose, she thought, almost choking at the boldly insulting—but more than slightly truthful—comparison. Thuận poked her tongue in her cheek to stifle the laughter that threatened. When she selected a needle threaded with the same Chinese red Thư had used, she let an irreverent giggle bubble out, in spite of herself.

Outside the shop, a golden day strolled by, but she didn't mind. After all, it was almost as bright indoors, surrounded as she was with gaily printed patterns and rainbow hues of vibrant silk threads. All this fanciful embroidery gave her endless hours of pleasure. It was more than just a job; it was a trade. A fine trade. A trade based on seven hundred years of proud, artistic tradition in Việt Nam.

Not like the sewing she used to do for Dì Ba.

An unexpected breeze stirred up pockets of cool and tossed them inside the open doorway. Thuận's forehead wrinkled as she sorted the threads of her memories.

Like prodding a sluggish water buffalo with a stick, Má had pushed her to ask Aunt Three for work. Barely bothering to mask her resentment, Thuận had volunteered at the small shop in Dì Ba's modest house where she cleaned, swept the floor, did anything and everything asked of her.

Once Thuận had proven her sincerity and worthiness, Aunt Three pointed at the large bags of free clothing she had collected from the American Red Cross. "You start here, Number Two," she said, addressing Thuận by her family position—eldest child ranked second to her parents.

Thuận snipped off buttons, removed zippers and carefully picked apart seams. After she freed the fabric, she flattened the pieces and sorted them by color and size. *All Americans must be giants,* she mused, *even the women and children. Much of this clothing can easily make two garments to fit one of us.* She considered the long-legged GIs who strode the streets and wharves of Sài Gòn. How they towered over the townspeople. Yes, they were giants. Giants who stalked the jungle, armed with weapons that spewed fire and death.

Thuận took no pleasure in deconstructing the used clothes. It was mindless work. It required no skill. It needed no artistry. Yet she did it, day after day, a farm ox yoked to work she despised.

At last, Aunt Three taught her how to thread and operate the treadle machine, giving her permission to do some simple sewing. "Seam lines only, like so. Keep your stitches even, Sister Two, and keep your seams straight. Slow. Straight. Even."

With an irritated toss of her head, Thuận began to sew. Without compensation. Until Aunt Three finally deemed her worthy of a few *dong* some weeks later.

After her skill at the machine sharpened and she began to immerse herself in the job, Thuận received regular pay. Before long, she learned the more intricate steps required to customize a fit by measuring point-to-point across the shoulders, figuring in length, allowing for seams and determining closures. Aunt Three taught her to convert those numbers into paper patterns on her own.

As adept as she became at sewing, Thuận despised the business itself. It was boring, tedious and certainly not what she hoped to do with her life. *You do, or you don't eat,* she mimed Má's mantra. Although necessity narrowed her choices as it did so many others in her country, she knew her hatred of sewing had colored her reasoning.

It served me well, she conceded grudgingly. She brought extra *dong* into the household while learning a skill Má swore would serve her well the rest of her life.

"Be grateful Fate offers you this opportunity," Má was quick to remind her when she complained.

Dì Ba had surprised her when, in addition to the tunics and pants they made and marketed in the village, she allowed Thuận to sew herself some new clothes. New clothes, too, for her sisters. And for her brothers. A bonus coconut-milk sweet.

Even so, if I never see another sewing machine, it will be fine by me!

So it was a bright day, indeed, when a friend met her one noon for lunch.

"The embroidery shop needs another worker." Dau's chopsticks toyed with a last grain of rice. "You would earn more *dong* for embroidery than sewing for Dì Ba."

Thuận's heart leapt at the idea. "More *dong*? Má can't object to that!"

She quit her job at Aunt Three's house with no remorse.

Fish and flamingoes. Bamboo and butterflies. Parrots, peacocks and pagodas. Embroidery introduced Thuận to an unexpected excitement over color and a newfound beauty in fabric and texture. Most of the scenes she transferred to fabric involved nature and sated a hollow spot somewhere deep inside her hungering soul.

Her quick mind and clever fingers feasted on the fancy stitches required, eager to grasp the intricacies necessary for such detailed workmanship. Up and down, one delicate thread at a time, she painted scenes as adeptly as any artist with a brush. A wooden stretcher was her easel and her canvas an endless supply of pillow tops, table runners, linen bedspreads, window dressings and silk tunics held taut in the table frame.

She never tired of the opportunity to ply her needle to items that would be sold at the upscale commercial markets in Sài Gòn—perhaps even shipped somewhere abroad. Tourists and wealthy patrons would purchase her delicate creations, even foreigners from exotic countries. Her fingers tingled at the possibility.

Cats and cranes. Lilies and lotus blossoms. With a few precise snips, Thuận clipped the tails of loose threads before loosening and removing the piece from its frame. She held it at arm's length to better admire the pure artistry of her handiwork.

Afternoon stretched and lengthened with the shadows. When the nagging ache in the back of her neck sharpened to a stab of pain, she used one hand to knead it while the other pierced the damask tablecloth with a fine needle, finished off the stitch and clipped the thread. Oblivious to the room full of girls whose mouths flew as fast as their nimble fingers, she smoothed another finished hornbill, considering it from several angles before setting it aside with a sense of achievement.

"Tonight Thuận? Can you come?" Dau called from across the room. "Thuận?"

"What?" She blinked, startled to note the dimness of late afternoon.

"Weren't you listening at all? I was asking if you could go tonight?"

"Go? Go where?"

"Into the city."

"With who?"

"With us." Dau indicated the entire room, arms spread as wide as a welcoming Buddha. "With all of us."

"Why?"

Dau shook her head in exasperation. "Why? To visit. To shop. To saunter through the park." She clicked her tongue. "Must there be a reason why? We've worked hard. Now it's time for play."

Thuận rotated her right shoulder, her head, her left shoulder—and shuddered involuntarily at the crackling in the bones of her upper spine. A reason why? There certainly were reasons enough why she should *not* go along with her friends. She could earn additional *dong* by carrying water for some neighbors yet this evening, or by meeting Má in the market to sell a few bowls of soup, or by doing chores for a shopkeeper or two, anything to turn a small profit. With the recent addition of another little mouth to feed at home, extra *dong* was more important than ever.

"Please, Thuận? Just this once?"

Thuận considered her friend's upturned nose and sparkling eyes. Thoughtfully, she glanced toward the doorway at the weighty rain clouds forming outside. Regardless of the turbulent Buddhist demonstrations recently disrupting life in Sài Gòn, she longed to do something more than just work. She ached to mingle in dense crowds along the streets of the city. To sit outside sipping tea with her friends. To gossip about neighbors and work and boys in long discussions that led anywhere and everywhere and only ended when they all scattered for home. A small smile flitted across her face.

In sudden decision, Thuận slipped her needle into a pincushion with enough force to override the stab to her conscience. Sliding her chair a few inches away from the table, she rose and smoothed her tunic. "I'm ready to go. Should we all walk? Or should we take a bus?" Work would, after all, still be there tomorrow.

A narrow bolt of lightning lit the heavens and throbbed like a nerve in the sky.

CHAPTER 5

American Military Base, 1967
Tân Sơn Nhứt, Việt Nam

The Wages of War

"Má, here is my earning for the week. I would like you to have this." Thuận bowed slightly at the waist, giving little thought to the ritual that was, by now, a natural occurrence. Cupped in her open palms was a paper folded around a short stack of *dong.*

Má accepted the respectful gift with a pleased nod and slipped it into her pocket. "Thank you, daughter. Fate has been kind."

Fate? Thuận's lips thinned, but a small tilt of her head acknowledged her mother's gratitude. The rhythm of her routines had begun to pain Thuận like a pebble in her sandal. Work pushed both edges of daylight, leaving little room for anything else in her life—especially friends. And Lác.

Tall, patient Lác. Until recently, she had only admired him like a brother, a protector.

"You boss me," he had teased one day, on the way home from the café where a group of their friends had met for tea.

"I don't."

"You do."

"No, I don't!"

"Of course you do," he said.

She lowered her eyes and looked at him through her thick lashes. "You're right. I do. And you like it!"

His face softened and he leaned toward her to whisper, "I do."

Their childhood friendship, deep and abiding, now had the flush of a delicate bud with petals waiting to unfurl. *Maybe someday, something more?* She blushed at the thought of a possible future together and wished only for more hours in her day to spend with him.

She hid her smile and looked at Má. Thuận took pride in her ability to meet her duty to family and found a measure of satisfaction each time she handed over her wages.

She cleared her throat. "I took a new job, Má."

"At Tân Sơn Nhứt?"

"Yes. In the officer mess hall."

"Good. The Chinese chef there is my friend. You will work hard for him."

As the war escalated, the number of American soldiers had grown, invading the South with their influence: sodas and music, makeup and hairspray, mini skirts and blue jeans. The influx also meant a surge of new jobs, jobs plentiful enough for everyone.

"War makes fine business," Thuận heard Ba say when he observed some of the shops change their names from French to American.

Doing anything for the military paid better than work she might get in Khánh Hội or even in Sài Gòn. With so many of their friends and neighbors finding employment, it felt natural that she follow suit.

Not long ago, Dau had traded her chair at the embroidery frame for a place in the kitchen at the Tân Sơn Nhứt Air Base and urged Thuận to join her.

"Think of the money you'll make, Number Two. It's about one hour distance by bicycle. We all ride the bus home at night."

"But so many are looking for work. I'm young. Inexperienced." Thuận nibbled the corner of her lower lip. "What if they won't hire me?"

"You are a good worker and old enough. Besides," Dau tapped her own chest, lowering an eyelid in a lazy wink, "you have a friend who works there. And that friend has friends who work there, friends who owe *me* favors."

"I will take any job, Dau, any job they might have." Hope rose inside her at the opportunity to better herself and earn more *dong*.

"I know there is an opening for dishwasher. You want an application? I can bring it back with me tomorrow."

The Military Assistance Command-Vietnam (MAC-V) sprawled at the northern edge of Sài Gòn where the Americans had built their compound at the end of the runway of Tân Sơn Nhứt, the commercial airport that served South Việt Nam.

Thuận pedaled her rusty bike to the mess hall. She eyed hovering helicopters, cargo planes landing on re-supply missions and sleek Voodoo fighters taking off on a mysterious mission of their own. Sturdy B-57 and B-52 bombers, parked with their noses straight ahead, waited to sniff out the enemy. Her eyes widened at the staging area for the scores of helicopters shuttling troops to and from the jungle. She craned her neck when GIs jumped out, coated with mud and sweat, to be quickly replaced by fresh soldiers wearing expressions that masked their emotions as surely as the camouflage covering their bodies.

Boys, the realization stunned her. *Why they're not much older than me.* She shook her head in dismay. *They are mere boys—fighting a war for a country not their own.* The revelation hung as heavy as evening fog.

The mess hall bustled with activity, from the two chefs and their six assistants to a battalion of dessert makers, salad makers and lowly dishwashers. Thuận did her work with such efficiency and thoroughness that she often offered to fill her extra time by mopping floors or preparing food. Impressed, one of the salad makers asked to have Thuận promoted to be her assistant.

Standards, Thuận discovered, were strict in the steamy kitchen. Not only did the officers expect their meals to be hearty and tasty, they also expected a fine presentation. The potential for artistry in food was a novel idea to Thuận, who tried her hand at the fancy garnishes: strawberry slices spread into a fan, radishes carved into rosettes, notched carrot rings pierced with asparagus spears and lime parings coiled into delicate flowers.

Almost like embroidery! The thought amused her.

One sticky afternoon, she sat on a stool at the countertop to trim the roots from a bundle of leeks. She clipped the green ends short and discovered a soothing sense of rhythm as, with a sharp paring knife, she made long, narrow slashes through the white bulbs. She plunged each leek into a bowl of ice water to curl the whites into bushy balls.

"Thuận?" The cook tapped her on the shoulder.

She wiped the sweat from her brow with a forearm and looked up with a smile. "Yes?"

"They want you to report to personnel right away."

She could see worry in the lines around his eyes. "Me? They want to see me? But, why?"

"They say you broke the rules."

"Rules? I've broken no rules. I do my work." She noticed a sudden stillness in the room.

The cook spread both hands, palms up. "I know nothing more."

Thuận wiped each finger of both hands with a damp cloth. She pushed her stool away from the countertop. Standing, she untied her apron and hung it on a hook by the door. Feeling a dozen pairs of curious eyes boring into her back, she lifted her shoulders, composed her features and left the safety of the kitchen.

The staccato of her heartbeat kept time with her clipped steps as she made her way across the base. She ignored wolf-whistles and grins from off-duty GIs and skirted the fellow who held a box radio near his ear, riveted to a loud broadcast of the Armed Forces Network.

What could be wrong? Her mind raced. *What rule could I have broken? Are there rules I don't know about? Will I lose my job?*

In the two short months since she began working at MAC-V, Thuận had made friends with the kitchen staff and, most recently, the dining-room staff. She liked them all, the waiters, the bussers, the housekeepers. Her family had come to rely heavily on her improved wages. Má and Ba were able to do more for the children and even handed Thuận a few *dong* each week to spend on herself. There was the strong possibility of another promotion soon.

Surely this is some kind of mistake. I must keep this job, I must! But she felt her hopeful fresh start at MAC-V threaten to shrivel and harden like old lemons.

Thuận smoothed her tunic with sweaty palms and took a deep breath before she stepped into the office.

"Huỳnh Thị Thuận? Are you Huỳnh Thị Thuận?" the interpreter asked.

Nodding, she whispered, "What is this? What is wrong?"

Before he could answer, the uniformed officer sitting behind a large desk narrowed his myopic eyes on the sheaf of papers he clenched and barked a short sentence. With a dip of his head, the interpreter turned to Thuận and began translating. "It has come to the attention of this office that you are not of age to work for us. It appears that you lied about your age on the application form."

"But I didn't lie!" The accusation stung. Thuận stretched her torso to make herself appear taller.

"Government regulations require all non-military employees to be sixteen years old."

"Sixteen? I am sixteen!" Thuận interrupted the interpreter and tugged on his shirt sleeve. "Please, tell him I am sixteen years of age."

The officer tapped firmly at a folder on his desk and scowled.

"He says the paperwork shows you're only fifteen-and-a-half," said the interpreter.

"Sixteen," Thuận insisted hotly, incensed that her integrity was at question. "*Sixteen*-and-a-half." She leaned forward and planted both palms on the desk to direct her spate of words to the officer himself, neither waiting nor caring that the interpreter struggled to keep up. "I tell you the truth. My day of birth is 1951, December 22. This is July 1967. You see? I am sixteen. What I say is true."

The interpreter held up his palm to halt her. "Wait. I see the problem. It's because of Chinese New Year. Let me explain so that he understands."

Thuận frowned. "What do you mean?"

"By American standards, a child turns one year of age on the actual day of her birth. Americans don't know that the people of Việt Nam calculate a first birthday at Tết, no matter when a child is born." He paused. "You see? You say you turned one in February of 1952. They say you turned one in December of 1952."

Thuận's eyes searched the two men as they discussed her situation. At last, the interpreter turned to her.

"He understands. The error is theirs."

Her hand flew to cover her heart. "Then . . . ?"

"You can continue to work—on a trial basis. Make just one mistake, though, and you'll be fired. Follow the rules, be on your best behavior, work hard and earn your keep. You understand?"

She gave a firm nod.

Like the layers of military invasion documented in papers at the corner newsstands, her life, too, had its own complexities. But understand she did. She knew how to follow regulations. She vowed to do absolutely nothing wrong, to make no mistakes, to work hard.

Hard work was, after all, what she understood best.

CHAPTER 6

Tết, 1968
Khánh Hội, Việt Nam

Dance of the Dragon

Thuận tossed restlessly on her woven sleeping mat. Packed as tightly as a flock of nestling chicks, she and nine others crowded the dirt floor of the small room they shared in their hut. Mostly, she never gave thought to her family's sleeping arrangements, but tonight the room felt close. Suffocating.

Thuận stared through the dark at the coconut-leaf roof and listened to the creaks as the house relaxed. From head to toe, she tingled with the excitement of tomorrow: Tết Nguyên Đán. The Lunar New Year. She felt grateful that the American military honored this holiday and allowed her time off from her job at MAC-V.

Má and Ba had, of course, insisted they begin the three-day celebration with a walk to Temple to light incense and pray at the urns of relatives who had gone ahead to meet their ancestors on the other side. There, they acknowledged their blessings and prayed for a successful future. They took advantage of the opportunity to forget the troubles of the past year, hopeful that the new one held the promise of better things to come. They paid homage to Buddha and made donations. Perhaps next time, with a toss or two of *keos*—coins—they would have their fortunes told.

My fortune, mused Thuận, *will it include Lác?* She was grateful for the breath of night that puffed through the unscreened window to cool the sudden heat seeping up her neck. Lately, it seemed her cheeks warmed at each thought of Lác.

Since her sixteenth birthday—according to American calculations—mere weeks ago, Thuận realized how much she appreciated the rituals that revolved around holidays. For the occasion of Tết, her family scrimped to enjoy the luxury of a few sweets: mangosteen, figs, squash and pumpkin strips, marinated in sugar and sun dried. Tết was a time for delicacies like sweet tamarind candies, tasty rice cakes wrapped in banana leaves and dry-roasted watermelon seeds, her personal favorite.

And the visits! Not to forget the visits, Thuận thought.

So many elders to see and to honor, grandparents, aunts and uncles. The second day of Chinese New Year was reserved for friends—Lác and Bính and many other former classmates, neighbors with large families of their own. From house to house to house she would visit tomorrow, as was customary.

"An khang thịnh vượng!" Her greeting would wish each friend peace and good health with hope for much prosperity ahead.

Later, they would continue the festivity by gathering in the city for the spiraling Dragon Dance. As brilliant as peacocks, the long-tailed creatures traditionally swirled through the streets of Sài Gòn to crashing cymbals and the frenzied beat of drums. She loved the way the over-sized dragons—rice-paddy green, glowing saffron and pumpkin orange—danced at the ends of bamboo poles twirled by costumed puppeteers. Why, they nearly took on lives of their own.

And the night sky!

This year, President Thiệu had reinstated the old traditions—including the wondrous firework displays that would bloom across the heavens in a brilliant spectrum of color and pattern. Red fragments from the spent fireworks would litter the streets, signaling prosperity, good luck and fresh, new beginnings.

Thuận remembered well how, as a little girl, she clamored to sit on Ba's shoulders for a panoramic view of the parade. From her lofty perch, the entire street was a swollen river of people. She had thought if she reached out she might actually touch the plump paper lanterns crisscrossing the streets.

Her newest brother whimpered across the room, an intrusive reminder that there were many younger than she now vying for that favored perch high on their father's shoulders.

Má stirred on her mat to comfort and soothe the baby. "Shhh, small one. All is well."

After a few minutes of rustling, the household settled and all Thuận heard were the deep sighs of untroubled sleep. The warmth of security and family wrapped around her. *Do dragons dance in their heads?* she wondered. She drifted back into the stillness, free to chase her thoughts once again.

More exciting than even the colorful Dragon Dance was the thought of the *Áo dài* she had selected with such care. She hesitated to imagine the breadth of Má's sacrifice to purchase traditional new clothes for her brood of children.

"Ah, but we must always greet the New Year with high expectations," Má had counseled.

Thuận shivered with delicious anticipation. What would Lác think of her white silk shirt? She loved how the delicate vines encircling its mandarin collar and the velvety-green water lilies, hand embroidered, trailed down a graceful pink stem.

After the New Year's celebrations, the tasteful tunic would be reserved for special occasions like weddings, holiday festivals and Temple. But that knowledge only made tomorrow sweeter, an opportunity to don the matching pants and float like a water lily before her classmates. Before Lác. If Fortune blessed them, someone would take a Polaroid of the entire group parading their finery.

She sighed in anticipation. Tomorrow promised new beginnings, the Year of the Monkey, 1968. She turned her head toward her clothing and stared through night's blackness where she knew it waited, folded neatly, atop a cardboard box by the door. A pristine beacon of promise and expectation.

Her lips curled in a soft smile and her eyelids drifted shut.

"Out children! Out! Run from the house!"

Thuận heard her parents' shrill yells even above the bedlam that suddenly surrounded her. Slammed against her. Filled her. She rolled from her straw mat in alarm. The sky belched mortars—one after another. Closer, and closer yet. The pound of heavy artillery howled across the dank pre-dawn.

"Run! Run!" parents shrieked into the fiery breath of war. Her parents. Other parents. Children screamed throughout the shipyard neighborhood as rocket-propelled grenades plowed into their homes.

When another explosion rocked the earth-packed floor beneath her bare feet, Thuận grabbed two wild-eyed brothers and dragged them toward the faint outline of the door. Without a break in her stride, she snatched up the silk *Áo dài*, clenching it under her arm.

Pulling the boys with her, she bolted into the chaos of the village street. Dust and smoke filled her lungs. Thuận gasped and choked back a cough. The strong smell of sulfur burned her nose; the acrid fumes of scorched plastic stung her eyes. In cruel imitation of Tết fireworks, menacing flares glowered over the western half of Sài Gòn.

Hands clenched in a human chain, she tugged her young brothers through the screaming throng. They cringed and ducked at each bombardment. Thuận scrambled to keep them together, close to the rest of their family, but the stampeding multitude swept her up.

She stumbled.

Jolted from behind, she fell to the ground. Sucked into a black pothole left by recent monsoons, Thuận sank to her knees.

"Wait for me!" she wailed when her small brothers, torn from her grip, were swept into the surging crowd. Miraculously, everyone veered around her. One of her sisters ran past. And another brother. A brilliant white explosive shrieked by. Thuận flung herself belly-down. Instinctively, she tucked her head under her arm.

The village, reduced to a rubble of leveled huts, reeked of singed bamboo and the unmistakable sickly-sweet stench of charred flesh. Everywhere around her, thatch smoldered. Dry wood burst into flames while industrial goods melted in an ooze of chemical sludge.

Her throat constricted. Her eyes watered. Her stomach heaved at the stink around her, on her, within her.

Thuận glanced to her right. In the sudden blaze of a burning building, she recognized him, lying several feet away, just out of reach.

"Lác!" His arm flayed out, palm up, stained brown with mud.

No. Not mud. Blood.

"Lác!" she screamed, stretching out a trembling hand. People coursed between them, blocking her view of his boyish face and wide, gentle eyes. But she knew. Deep in her young girl's heart, she knew.

"Lác," she repeated, this time in a whisper, and felt a gaping hole in her soul where his spirit once dwelled.

Another grenade exploded nearby. Bequeathing Lác to his ancestors, Thuận staggered to her feet and plunged into the panicked crowd that muscled her forward. She left her *Áo dài*—along with her dreams—trampled and stained in the mud-rutted road.

No dragons would dance tomorrow.

CHAPTER 7

American Central Command Post, 1969
Long Bình, Việt Nam

Faces

Even more than a year later, Thuận shuddered to remember the hours and months following the Tết Offensive. For several days, she had crouched with thousands of others at a temporary shelter set up near the waterfront while the ground vibrated with the enraged roar of battle. In the City of Tents, they crowded side by side with strangers and slept sitting up, the war at their backs. She had covered her ears with her hands to muffle the thunder of rockets, bombs and bazookas. More fortunate than many, her family was able to reunite there, each member accounted for. Safe and whole.

Others joined them by the scores, refugees from the embattled southern quarter of Sài Gòn, escaping the crossfire between government troops and Việt Cộng sapper squads who punctuated the days and nights by setting off explosives.

Rockets and grenades continued to lay waste to the area in fierce street combat. Terror-stricken parents babbled on and on about the dead and injured who littered the sidewalks and the house-to-house fighting and the paratroopers who advanced through the deserted suburbs engaging Việt Cong battalions and about the American soldiers who carried children to safety past rubble and carnage.

Every face, whether foreign or familiar, mirrored the same horror and suffering.

Finally allowed to return to Khánh Hội, Thuận's family helped neighbors pick through the rubble, hoping to salvage enough to rebuild. Their own two-room house was unharmed. Fortune? Luck? The grace of God?

She shrugged. The loss of Lác, gentle Lác, made her think less kindly of a god who could turn his face from life. And death. A god who could turn away from the fate of her country and its people. The memory of Lác lying in the street, his vibrant face closed and still, was another round of mortars ripping through the core of her.

Only a few months later, before they could even clear the rubble, a barrage of rockets had slammed into the heart of Sài Gòn and signaled the beginning of a second offensive. A mini-Tết. This time, fighting started at the northeast edge of the city where Communist troops seized the highway bridge and attacked the air base at Tân Sơn Nhứt. Destruction stalked the city riddled with mines and booby traps that wounded civilians and killed innocent children in the heavily populated areas.

Thuận steadied her trembling hand and shook her head to rid it of the images.

She was grateful for her new job at Long Bình. The mandated post-Tết curfew had made commuting to and from the kitchen at MAC-V cumbersome. Although troops continued to patrol the city, sniper bullets still raked the streets and increased the danger and dread of traveling.

The rat-a-tat of gunfire had heightened her anxiety on a daily basis. Was it close? How close? Too close? Should she get off her bike? Or pedal faster to get to the base?

Until Tết, the bite of war seemed no more bothersome than a pesky mosquito, Thuận thought. But with the conflict now at her doorsill, it was no longer possible to ignore her country's politics and battles.

At every kiosk, headlines screamed the casualties: A half-million refugees—fleeing bombed villages and burning ruins—flooded Sài Gòn in a deluge of hungry humanity seeking food, safety and shelter. Fear was the most telling feature on their faces. The empty eyes of street orphans haunted Thuận's dreams. And the sudden loss of her nearly war-oblivious girlhood pierced her conscience as deeply as the barb of the Punji sticks set to penetrate the boots of enemy soldiers.

When the Chinese chef at MAC-V took a position at the military base farther north and invited her to accompany him as an assistant, Thuận jumped at the opportunity and the advancement. The dwindling pangs of homesickness were a small price to pay for a measure of newly earned independence, the freedom of dormitory life at Long Bình with the other girls and the excitement of new friends and new challenges.

The Central Command Post at Long Bình was built like a huge fortress surrounded by walls, fences and barbed wire. Housed within it, Thuận discovered a hospital and a stockade—fondly dubbed "The LBJ" by the infantrymen—and quickly learned her way around the airstrip, dormitories and officers' clubs. She appreciated the progression she had already made there, from assistant to cook to waitress, and certainly the hefty tips that came with her new position at the small officers' club everyone called Annex 19. Already she understood more English and had mastered enough simple phrases to get by on base.

However, several months earlier, her American boss at the Main Officers' Club struggled with the cultural differences and the problems he faced communicating with his civilian employees. He finally handled it his own way.

Tall and attractive, Captain John had growled in frustration.

"I swear you girls all look alike. Same black hair. Same dark eyes." His uniformed arm swept the room to include cooks and cocktail waitresses. "You even dress so much alike, I can't tell you apart."

Thuận's head snapped around at the odd comment. One of her friends hid a snicker. *You really think that?* Thuận's brow wrinkled in dismay. *What do you mean, you can't tell us apart? That's ridiculous. We can tell!*

"And your names! They all sound the same. I can't wrap my teeth around them and I sure as hell can't remember them." He squinted at the ceiling for a long moment, two deep furrows at the corners of his mouth. "Tell you what, girls. Let's make this easy." He pointed a slender finger at Thuận. "You there. You look like a Tammy. Yep. I think you're going to be Tammy."

Did he say Tah-mee? Tah-mee? Thuận rolled the new name around the inside of her mouth, sampling it—and liking the exotic taste.

"Tammy." Captain John nodded, obviously pleased with his choice. "It's from a song, you know." He hummed the melody. "Ta-a-mmy, Ta-a-mmy, Tammy's in love." He sang a phrase or two in a surprisingly agreeable baritone.

Tah-mee. The strangeness tickled her tongue. *An American name for a teenage girl in Việt Nam.* Oddly, she was pleased with the novel idea.

"Is that okay by you?" Captain John's eyes, the intense blue of a pitta bird's wing, crinkled upward at the corners.

Thuận noticed how the light glistened on the top of his head. The strands of hair were the liquid gold of the Pabst Blue Ribbon that flowed at the bar. She smiled shyly into his ruggedly handsome face and nodded her agreement.

Captain John pointed to another worker. "You there, you'll be Susie. And you'll be Jane." He worked his way through the staff, testing names with the fervor of an expectant mother. He wore his smug satisfaction like a medal.

Now, fully accustomed to her American name, Tammy looked around Annex 19. The canteen was busy. Noisy. Rowdy. A typical Saturday night with thirsty infantrymen swarming the club, drawn by a common, but elusive, hope: band music loud enough to squelch their memories and alcohol potent enough to drown their nightmares. They shouldered a spot at the bar and jostled each other for a seat at tables that filled as quickly as they emptied.

Tammy placed another order with the bartender and picked up the drinks already waiting. Steadying a full tray of glasses, she threaded her way through the crowd, hardly noticing the heavy haze of cigar and cigarette smoke that clouded the room. She dodged an amorous hand and tossed back good-natured refusals to several sly offers.

"You wan foo? I ge foo. You wan lik-ker? I ge lik-ker. You wan Tah-mee?" She tossed her head. "Fo-get ih, GI!"

It hadn't taken her long to learn how to handle these boisterous soldiers, these boys playing at war. She pressed through the herd of randy bulls to a table in the far corner where she handed out the round of drinks.

One fellow picked up the glass in front of him and sniffed. "What the hell? I didn't order this," he objected.

"You or-rur, you pay," Tammy insisted.

"Not me, missy. I just got here. This must belong to the guy who just left." He jerked a thumb toward the door and handed the shot glass to her.

Tammy's eyes narrowed in suspicion. "You diff-ren guy?"

"Must be." He smirked and elbowed the man sitting next to him.

She could swear the soldier who had been sitting there a mere five minutes earlier had the same blond hair, the same blue eyes, the same open-throated shirt.

"Wha you nam?" Her voice was full of doubt.

"John."

"You nam John?" Tammy squinted through the haze of smoke. "*He* nam John, too. You *all* nam John."

She plopped the glass back on the tray snugged in the crook of her arm and swallowed a theatrical sigh. "Wha you wan or-rur . . . John?"

With an irritated slap of her high-heeled sandals, she clicked her way back toward the bar to get his drink, muttering to herself all the way. It was, after all, a common mistake, one most of the girls made. It simply couldn't be helped. These soldiers all dressed alike. They all looked alike. They even had the same name. John, John, John.

Huh.

Was it any wonder the cocktail waitresses couldn't tell them apart?

CHAPTER 8

Evacuation Hospital, 1969
Long Bình, Việt Nam

Grim Realities

It wasn't until after a heavy rain scoured off the thick layers of dust that Tammy had discovered a large, red cross emblazoned on the white roofs of each hospital ward—wards which, themselves, formed the shape of large Xs. They were adjacent to the Dust-Off Unit for the Med-Evac helicopters that extracted casualties from the battlefield.

Composed of a few dozen buildings, the 93rd Evacuation Hospital occupied the north corner of the base: the operating room, emergency room and laboratory; quarters for EMs, doctors and nurses; separate Quonset huts for headquarters, quartermasters and company clerk; and, of course, the central materials section, showers and mess hall. There was an outdoor theater arena where the medical staff gathered most evenings to watch movies.

None of it impressed Tammy much; it was simply there, cluttering the landscape. In a military installation the size of Long Bình, the 93rd Evacuation Hospital was only a fraction of the bigger picture. What happened inside its walls, however, was another matter.

Each time she had a break from her cocktail waitressing, Tammy found herself walking to the nearby wards to spend a few minutes, sometimes thirty minutes, at other times a full hour. Time had a way of slipping by within the doors of those units where death and disability wandered freely.

The nurses, both male and female, were genial. Occasionally, they requested her volunteer services to translate for a Vietnamese patient. Even with her still-developing language skills, she could act as a go-between—if the staff simplified the questions they asked her to repeat and if she did the same with the patients' responses.

Tammy created a useful niche for herself by helping at the hospital. But that wasn't what drew her back, time and time again.

She went because of the patients.

Stripped of the weaponry they wore like Chợ Lớn tea girls wore makeup, the soldiers were reduced to the kind of boys she once knew at school. Except these boys were lost. Confused. Injured.

Most of them appeared to be her age, although at times it was difficult to believe. Vacant eyes stared from battle-scarred faces perched atop bodies swathed in white bandages that oozed blood and pus. Some turned their heads away, unwilling or unable to engage in conversation, trying to maintain a firm grip on their emotions . . . and reality. Hardship and horror seared their souls as surely as Agent Orange destroyed the lush countryside of Việt Nam. They were boys with a past too horrific to explain and a future so remote, so indistinct—so improbable—many expressed an uncertainty that it could exist.

Other patients seemed even younger. If that was possible. Too young to be fighting a war, their eyes pleading forgiveness and, at the same time, begging. Begging for . . . what? Love? Understanding? Uncomplicated human kindness?

Their fingers clawed and clung, reluctant to release their grip on hers.

Tammy glanced down and inspected her hands, small and dainty, like the rest of her. Yet strong. Strong and capable. She splayed her slender fingers and examined the taut muscles, marveling at the power they were capable of wielding.

Power to console.

Power to comfort.

Power to calm.

She had learned that touch—personal touch—was powerful enough to convey the kind of loving care and support family members give to one another. When they are present to give it.

Which isn't the case now, is it?

These injured soldiers were far from home; they had left their families behind to come to this alien place. As had she.

We only have each other, she thought.

She grasped the doorknob to steel herself, stepped inside the ward and bumped into a medic.

"'Scuze me, Miss." He reached out to steady her but didn't slow his steps. "Are you all right?"

Before she could answer, he was out the door.

Her gaze swept the open, bustling room with its hectic insensitivity to privacy. So many patients, so little time. She headed toward the bed closest to the door. A quick scan told her the soldier was in bad shape, but Tammy didn't avert her eyes. She couldn't. There was something about the dark side of the war—grisly, gory and gruesome—that held a fascination, a kind of morbid fascination, for her. The splattered blood that repelled her friends and coworkers somehow intrigued Tammy.

She approached the patient without hesitation.

The man's good eye stared, gauging her reaction. The rest of his face was wrapped and bound, except for the hole, the hole where his jaw used to be. She could see his teeth through the wired apparatus that appeared to be holding his face together.

Determined not to betray his condition by a grimace, Tammy forced an unperturbed expression and smiled pleasantly at the soldier. Was he Vietnamese? American? It was impossible to tell. She gave his good hand a gentle squeeze and chose an English greeting.

"He-llo."

He glanced at her from the corner of his eye, then looked away. Although he blinked a few times, he kept his gaze averted.

She tried again. "He-llo."

He hissed wordlessly through the gaping hole.

She leaned toward him. "Wha you say?"

The man looked beyond her, through her, refusing to acknowledge her presence.

Tammy kept his hand in hers. Simply waiting. Without a word, she stood at his side, looking past his pain, past his infirmities, past his anger. She caressed his hand, still waiting. She was in no hurry.

Feeling a slight movement from his fingers, she glanced again at his face and marveled—even with all the bandages, she could see that he had softened. A glow lit his eye; the exposed skin around the socket eased, smoothed. Tammy squeezed again, but before she could loosen her grip, his hand curled until he could lace his fingers with hers. With a deep sigh, the wounded warrior closed his eye.

Tammy stayed at his bed, listening until she heard his breathing even. When she was certain he was asleep, she carefully freed her hand and turned to the patient in the cot next to his.

A giggle threatened to erupt, in spite of her efforts to suppress it.

This sleeping soldier had the bald head of a Buddha. The smooth gray of his eyelids and the rounded mound of his belly, wrapped with thick dressings, further enhanced the comparison. She scanned the length of him.

"I'm one long drink of water, ain't I?"

Tammy jumped.

A grin widened his lips and puckered his cheeks before he opened his eyes, the promising green of sprouting rice. "My momma taught me to stand when a lady enters the room, my momma did." He gave her a lazy wink. "Good she's not here to see me shirking my manners."

He lifted his two bandaged hands. "Sorry. Can't even offer you a proper handshake with these paws." He gave a woeful shake of his head. "Not with these paws."

Tammy's response was an uncertain smile. "How you fee, GI?"

"Name's Hank, Ma'am. Call me Hank. And I feel like crap, Miss Sunshine, like crap." He cleared his throat. "My momma wouldn't approve the way my language's deteriorated, either."

"You mah-mah goo lay-dee?"

"Yeah." His voice went flat. "Yeah, she's a good lady, my momma. Too good for what I've become in this hell-hole."

Tammy gave his shoulder a squeeze and leaned close to whisper, "You goo, too, GI. You goo son. You goo GI."

The soldier blinked rapidly and lowered his head.

A stir nearby caught her attention. She gave Hank's arm a lingering pat and moved to the foot of his bed where she watched a nurse bent over a patient directly across the aisle. The nurse finished changing the dressing and walked away, forgetting to replace the sheet over the young man.

He was in bad shape. Unconscious. Lots of tubes crisscrossing his chest. Tubes going in. Tubes going out. Tammy's eyes wandered lower and widened at the size of the fresh bandages he wore. A small frown pinched her forehead. Something looked odd, out of place.

A strangled gasp escaped her throat. No wonder he looked so peculiar. The fresh dressing near his middle swaddled the young man's thighs—or what was left of them. He was missing the lower half of his body.

Stumps.

He has stumps for legs.

Her hands tightened on the metal frame of the bed as she pressed the knuckles of one fist to her mouth. She closed her eyes to gather her composure.

"Land mine," Hank muttered from behind her. "They steal more limbs than a fox steals chickens. And just as sneaky, too."

Tammy set her jaw and gritted her teeth against the injustices of this war that ruled—and robbed—them all of lives and limbs. She couldn't stop staring at the soldier's disfigurement.

Half a man, half a life. What a high price to pay. She moaned.

Sweat beaded her forehead, popped out on her upper lip. Feeling lightheaded, she leaned against Hank's bed to steady herself and swallowed the brackish bile stinging her throat. Tammy wiped her forehead with the back of her wrist.

She stepped into the middle of the aisle.

She knew the legless GI needed someone at his side. Someone to reassure him, someone to whisper platitudes, someone to hold his hand and wipe his brow and utter words of encouragement and concern and support and . . .

Yes, he desperately needed somebody. But it wouldn't be her. Not today.

Feeling a backwash of tears, Tammy turned and raced from the ward.

CHAPTER 9

Annex 19, 1970
Long Bình, Việt Nam

Casualties

"Are you still worried about Daniel?" asked Susie. With an ease and adeptness Tammy admired, the barmaid poured a shot of bourbon and set the glass on a tray.

"Someone told me he was sent out on maneuvers for a week. Well, it's been more than two weeks now and I still haven't seen him come in." Tammy reached for the tray. "Are you sure he hasn't been here?"

Flicking her narrow wrist, Susie mopped a puddle on the bar top. "Not yet. You like him?"

Tammy shrugged. "He's just a friend."

Susie rolled her eyes. "You and I are friends. You and Tau are friends. But, calling Daniel a friend? Somehow, I think he's more."

Ducking her head to smother a grin, Tammy turned away to deliver the drink to her customer.

Friendships between working civilians flourished at Annex 19. The intimacy of the small bar and grill, housed on the first floor of the barracks, encouraged casual relationships. Susie and Tammy loved to gossip and banter, and the GIs had no clue what they were saying. None of them understood a word of Vietnamese. Nor did their likeable, lenient boss, Billy—who was too busy showering Susie with attention to care about their girlish chatter.

But, was Daniel a friend?

Tammy only knew him as a good customer, one who stood out from the rest. Unlike so many of the enlisted men on base, he was never rude and showed no signs of crudeness. She had served him several sandwiches, brought him many drinks during the months of his tour of duty. No big deal. Daniel tipped well, smiled politely back when she greeted him and was quick to laugh and joke. Overall, he was a nice fellow.

Yes, he was a friend.

A friend who just happened to have skin bronzed the warm shade of ginger and a thick mat of curls that peeked from the deep vee of his shirt, partially unbuttoned in summer's swelter. Daniel had the topaz eyes of a cat and . . . Tammy's palms flew to her cheeks, hiding the heat creeping across them.

As she headed back to the bar with more orders to fill, she saw Daniel walk in. He yanked at a chair in the far corner and hunkered down, his back against the wall. His wavy blond hair darkened in the dim light.

Detouring to his table, Tammy ignored the requests of her other customers, pretending she didn't hear them.

"He-llo." She kept her voice cheery, but neutral.

Daniel barely glanced up.

"You wan dree?"

She took his scant nod for a yes. But, while she waited at the bar for Susie to pour, Tammy couldn't keep her eyes off him.

"Something's wrong with Daniel."

Susie set a Pabst on the tray. "How do you know?"

"Something is . . . different about him tonight. See that frown knotting his forehead? And he's so quiet. Whatever is wrong, it's serious." Leaving behind the tray full of drinks, she grabbed his glass and wove between tables until she came to him.

In one fluid motion, she pulled out a chair, sat down and placed the beer in front of him. Tammy folded her arms on the table and leaned on her elbows toward Daniel. "You sic?"

Lashes, long and thick, shuttered his eyes. "No."

"You o-kay?"

He picked up the beer and tossed it back. With exaggerated gentleness, he set the glass on the table, meticulously centering it in a whitened ring from old condensation. He refused to look at her.

"You wan moe?"

When Daniel didn't answer, Tammy shrugged and pushed back her chair. Other men were waiting for their drinks.

Throughout her evening shift, Tammy laughed with customers, took orders for burgers, served more rounds than she could count and pocketed her tips. She kept a distant vigilance on the far wall where Daniel nursed a second drink, his face tight, discouraging any overtures, dampening any conversation.

When the kitchen closed for the night, the crowd thinned. Most of the men had already gone upstairs to their bunks; and the few left were playing cards or downing a final beer. Tammy, waiting for a ride back to the dormitory, dangled on a bar stool, one leg swinging idly, chatting while Susie wiped glasses. Without warning, she heard loud words behind her, obviously deprecations although they were hurled with such speed and ferociousness she couldn't decipher them.

By the time she whipped around to face the room, Daniel stood toe-to-toe with another GI. Fists balled, the two men glared at each other, their angry words getting progressively more belligerent. Daniel glanced up at her gasp. Muttering an oath under his breath, he lowered his hands and strode out the door. Stunned, the other soldier hesitated.

"What the hell!" he bellowed and barreled after Daniel.

Tammy swung back to the bar. "What was that about?"

"Who knows? It doesn't take much to spark a fight around here." Susie braced her arms against the counter. "Haven't you noticed? These infantrymen have tempers as explosive as fireworks at Chinese New Year!"

"Where do you suppose they went?"

Susie shrugged. "They probably took their argument outside."

Tammy stared at the door, willing Daniel to return. Her fingers thrummed the countertop. Her teeth nibbled the corner of her lips. When she couldn't bear waiting and worrying a minute longer, she hopped off the bar stool. "I'm going to look for him."

The entry light outside Annex 19 spilled in a wide halo. Night air hung heavy and sultry and quiet. Tammy stepped into the black beyond, probing the deep shadows beside the complex. She found Daniel a few yards away, leaning against the wall of the barracks, his dejected profile barely discernible in the dark.

"You o-kay?" she half-whispered.

"I'm okay."

He didn't look okay.

She edged closer. "You shure o-kay?"

"I said I'm fine," he mumbled.

Tammy searched his silhouetted features. "Go in-sigh." She reached for his hand and tugged. "Go in-sigh," she urged again.

Daniel didn't bother to pull away. He let Tammy nudge him along a couple of steps until—without warning—he stopped and drew her into his muscled arms, burying his face into the soft skin exposed at her nape. He nuzzled closer, his breath hot against her hair.

Startled, Tammy pulled back. But before she could break away, Daniel leaned into her. His chest heaved against hers and his embrace tightened and . . .

. . . and she felt the damp smear of his tears on her neck.

He muffled a strangled sob.

Instinctively, Tammy enfolded the breadth of him in her arms and she widened her stance to bear his weight when the tall soldier collapsed against her. Weeping.

Weeping?

Never before had Tammy seen any of these rough-and-tumble soldiers, brave defenders of liberty, break down and cry. They were all bluster and brawn, these men, as quick to fight each other as they were to fight the enemy.

Tough? Yes.

Mean? Yes.

Coarse? Yes.

But soft enough to shed tears? Not that she had ever witnessed.

Something terrible must have happened to Daniel on the battlefield, she realized. *Maybe the death of a . . .* she faltered over the word . . . *a friend?*

Daniel's sobs were a wretched cry from the heart that she recognized. His tears signaled the gut-wrenching pain of deep loss, the kind of loss she had felt when Lác died during the Tết Offensive.

Realization dawned with unflinching clarity: War meant loss—not only for the soldiers of her country, but for the Americans as well. Americans whose deaths seared holes in the souls of mothers, fathers, brothers and sisters. In families.

Families—just like hers? The thought made her pause.

So many casualties. So many lives altered. How many Vietnamese had died? How many nameless GIs?

And what might yet happen to those men whose names she was beginning to know?

American bosses, American acquaintances. American . . . friends.

This war chews up young men by the handful and spits out the hulls.

She thought back to Hank and the hundreds of injured troops like him who were delivered to the hospital wards every day by air ambulances. She remembered how she had shuddered and run from the sight of the legless GI.

Still deeply ashamed of the weakness she had exhibited in the hospital, Tammy lifted her chin. *This time,* she resolved, *I'll stand my ground.*

Daniel's weight pressed against her. With a catch in her throat, Tammy gripped her friend's wracking shoulders and drew him closer to her breast. Her eyes clouded as she mourned for his heartbreak and for her own.

At that moment, Tammy could only think of one thing to do. She squeezed her arms around Daniel to absorb some of his pain and sorrow. And cried with him.

CHAPTER 10

Apothecary Shop, 1971
Sài Gòn, Việt Nam

Counter Offensive

The bullet-scarred wall was a backdrop for the young boy who played soldier in front of it. He aimed a toy rifle at his own shadow. Pretending to shoot and take a hit, he fell to the ground in a convincing writhe.

Tammy winced and crossed the road to avoid the building and the scene.

A bitter reminder of the intense street fighting that gripped Sài Gòn during the Tết Offensive nearly three years earlier, the pocked graffiti reflected the holes in her soul. Although she'd spent her entire life in a country fraught by war, she only recently began to see the possibilities of so much more.

Her encounters with Americans, in combination with newly earned job skills at Long Bình, gave her sips of hope that there was something better out there—somewhere—for her. That she could believe again in her own future. That she could be something . . . be something . . . well, be something greater.

Greater than herself. Greater than the trailing wisps of a dream she kept buried in the secret chambers of her heart.

Tammy passed street traders, conical hats slanted against the afternoon sun like the parasols at Vũng Tàu Beach, balancing on their haunches, arms resting loosely on upbent knees, selling. Always selling. Wooing shoppers with a bowl of fragrant fish soup or a cup of brewed tea in exchange for enough *dong* to purchase something different for their own families to eat.

Need a haircut?

Your fortune told?

Your tooth filled?

Your shoes repaired?

How about a fine duck, a fat swine, a live snake?

When she felt the buildings begin to thicken as dense as elephant grass, Tammy hurried across the bridge, determined to finish her errands before it was time to catch the bus back to the army base. She angled across the busy street.

A bicyclist jangled his bell in warning and she scooted from his path. Deciding there was no need to fight the herd of mopeds and cyclos that clogged Sài Gòn's main thoroughfare, she ducked through the doorway of a local apothecary to make the final purchase on her shopping list.

The abrupt coolness of the store raised bumps on her bare legs. Tammy folded her arms close to her chest, shivering as she wandered the tight aisles. Idly, she read a few labels, compared prices and fingered some new items. She tidied a short stack of cartons threatening to spill into the narrow aisle.

Enough, she scolded herself. *Find what you came after so you won't have to run to the bus stop like last time.*

She made her selection and moved toward the busy young woman rearranging the display behind the counter.

"Hello," the woman greeted her customer. "Is this all you need today, or might I . . ." Her voice trailed off. "Thuận? Is it you? Is it really you?" She nearly squealed her excitement. An open smile crimped her sculpted cheeks.

Tammy's eyes widened in recognition. "Phượng?"

Phượng bobbed her head. "How long is it since I've seen you, Chị cả?" she asked with the ease of familiarity rooted in childhood. "It's been years, I think. Eight or nine at least. Not since our school days, I'm sure!"

Tammy cringed and stalled before clearing her throat. "Grade Five. I haven't seen you since just after Grade Five." She was startled to discover that the thorny memory had left a scar.

"Well, it's been a long while, that I know. Too long! Much too long." Phượng looked so professional in her crisply tailored pharmacist coat.

"Fortune has smiled on you, I see."

"Yes, I've held this position for awhile now." Her rouged lips pursed in a half-smile. "And you? What have you been doing all this time?" She straightened the lapel of her pristine-white jacket.

Tammy stilled her own hands with effort. They itched to tug at the black mini skirt she wore. Why had she chosen it today of all days? "Oh, you know. A job here, a job there. Helping Má in the market. Embroidery. Whatever work I can find." She adjusted her wildly flowered top, in spite of herself.

Tammy watched as Phượng smoothed an imaginary loose strand in her sophisticated up-do, her manicured nails catching the light, shiny and sleek, the fiery red of a dragon's breath. Tammy curled her own fingers until the nails bit into her palms.

"Why haven't you stopped in here before, Chị cả? I haven't seen you around anywhere."

Tammy looked away, composing herself. "I work outside of the city."

"Oh, where?"

"Long Bình. For the American military."

With eyes as wise and worldly as a Sài Gòn city sister, Phượng examined her friend from head to high-heeled sandals with deeper interest. "What is it like, working for the Americans?"

"Well, the men are plentiful. Some are very nice looking. And they all like to flirt!" Tammy kept her comments lighthearted, but, as the two chattered on, she wanted only to escape this waking nightmare.

Why her and not me? The pain Tammy felt was as honed as Má's fish-boning knife. *Phượng is so accomplished. She stands behind the counter, not in front of it. But she's not any smarter than me. That, I know . . . I'm the one who fed her the answers at school!*

And, for what? Rice. Bananas. Anything to silence the rumble in a small child's belly. While Phượng's parents had the means to support their daughter's goals, to further their daughter's education, her own insisted she shoulder the weighty mantle of Eldest Child.

Not that she begrudged her friend's obvious success, but the memory of a young girl's dream—and despair—painted a broad swath that stained this chance meeting.

Was Phượng an apprentice? An assistant? An herbalist? Tammy really didn't care to know. It was obvious that she had a promising career. A career instead of a job. Phượng had furthered her education and become someone to be proud of. She became the woman Tammy thought she, herself, could become.

Would become.

Should become.

"And your parents, how are they?" Phượng's eyes searched those of her friend's while her conversation continued to be genial, good-natured and irritatingly thoughtful as she inquired about each member of Tammy's large family and brought up stories of school days, old acquaintances and celebrations past.

Covering her bitterness like a stain on her shirt, Tammy kept a cheerful lilt in her voice. *After all,* she scolded, *my problem is about* me, *not about her.*

When she could comfortably interrupt the flow of the conversation, Tammy pointed out that her purchase wasn't yet completed. "I must catch the bus back to the base before curfew," she reminded her classmate. "I want to keep my job." She forced a small smile.

Phượng handed her the shopping bag. "Stop in again soon!" Her invitation was as warm as her parting embrace. "And next time you're near Sài Gòn, we will make time for a long visit, perhaps a nice meal in the city."

Tammy's goodbye sounded stiff, even though she tried her hardest to make it natural. She rushed from the store and crossed the street without looking, unflinching when a moped swerved to avoid her. As she neared the bridge, she stopped and slumped against the wall of a building for support, one icy hand planted flat against its sun-drenched warmth.

How effortless it had been for Phượng to smile and act natural. Tammy closed her eyes. *No wonder. Just look at the ease of her life!*

Phượng had never slapped away the grasping paws of drunk GIs or cooked in the steamy kitchen of a mess hall or stood for hours up to her elbows in greasy dishwater. She had never bent over an embroidery frame until her fingers cramped and her neck complained. She had never sat for long days, picking apart the seams of musty old clothing, one tiny stitch after another.

Tammy worked herself up until she was jealous enough to spit needles.

Phượng never peddled food in the market, a fish at a time. Or carried an entire shop across her shoulder to cook and sell in the street, basket and charcoal burner swaying on a bamboo pool.

With her thoughts still spewing venom, Tammy pushed herself away from the wall and paced.

For certain, Phượng never hauled buckets of water, too heavy for young arms.

Or slopped swine.

Or shoveled their dung.

"Hoink! Hoink!" Tammy spat the words like a curse. Suddenly aware that she had said them aloud, she spun around to see if anyone heard. She felt her cheeks flame.

Oh, yes, Fortune had definitely dealt a fine hand to her old classmate.

Tammy stared, unblinking, at the pesky buzz of American Hueys speckling the sky overhead. Her gaze drifted lower and focused on the side of raw pork hanging outside the hole-in-the-wall shop next door. Flies darted and droned around the carcass.

She shook her head to clear it of all this nonsense and eased back into the tidal wave of people heading home from work. Or back to work. Or looking for work. Always work, work, work.

Fighting the current of humanity and self pity that threatened to suck her under, she bobbed up and down through its shifting ebb and flow, a lost sampan in rough waters. Tammy expelled a long breath in a vain attempt to slow her pounding pulse even as she raced against time toward the bus. Toward her job. Toward her own destiny.

I'm nothing but a small stone, she thought, *caught in the undertow, dashed against hard rocks, waiting to be tossed from the turbid river bottom onto the bank.*

Almost panting as she boarded the bus for Long Bình, Tammy found an empty space at the rear and plopped down on the bench. She closed her burning eyes, trying not to replay the scene with Phượng. Even so, it ran through her mind again and again, like the reels of John Wayne movies the GIs watched on base.

She forced her thoughts toward tomorrow. There was the storeroom to check, a shipment to unpack, invoices to process. A long, shuddering sigh shook her body and forced its way out her mouth.

Tammy could have sworn she heard Má's sensible voice. "Do what you need to do, my daughter. Just do."

Tammy's lips thinned. As stubborn as a fighting fish that couldn't let go of the bait, she wrestled a few more minutes with her envy of Phượng. *Oh, I'll do what I need to do, Má,* she vowed. *Phượng did it. So can I!*

She squinted out the window of the bus, deep in thought.

CHAPTER 11

NCO Club, 1971
Long Bình, Việt Nam

Taking Inventory

Turning so the showerhead sprayed against her back, Tammy curved her shoulders forward to ease the tightness. Her spine felt the effects from carrying tonight's extra-heavy trays. The NCO Club had been crowded and the men so generous with their tips that she lost count of how many drinks she had served.

With a tremendous sigh of satisfaction at the extra money she could give Má and Ba this Sunday, Tammy sudsed her long hair and leaned to let the cloudburst thrum against her scalp. She felt it sluicing down her face to wash away the lingering stench of cigarettes and Pabst Blue Ribbon that seemed to seep into her pores.

"Ummm." She basked in the moist heat, reveling in the decadence of water and warmth.

A giggle erupted with a suddenness that surprised her.

"This is a luxury I've started taking for granted," she half-scolded the empty room. "A luxury I never want to give up."

Bathing in Khánh Hội had involved toting a bucket of well water to the crude outbuilding her family sometimes shared with neighbors. Because soap was a precious commodity, an extravagance actually, she made do by merely rinsing herself with the water she scooped with a coconut bowl and poured over her body. At times, everyone in the district went outside to wash themselves in the drenching monsoons that pounded the earth during the rainy season. But that, too, was usually completed without soap. While fully dressed.

By contrast, the memory of her first hot shower in the dormitory was stark. Water had gushed from the walls with a mere turn of the tap and steam billowed to fill the five-spigot stall, a stall so generously large it could accommodate several bathers at one time. And all this, without any effort on her part.

Fortune had finally found her.

Now, Tammy reddened as she recalled the awe she'd felt a few years earlier. Her friend Dau needed to explain and demonstrate the flush toilet in the officers' mess hall back at MAC-V—a far cry from the small platform that straddled the creek running under the bamboo outbuilding at home.

Dau chuckled at Tammy's amazement. "I felt the same as you the first time I saw this!"

They had stood in the washroom during their break that afternoon. Taking turns, they flipped the toilet handle again and again, simply to watch the magic happen. And every time, they held their hands over their mouths to stifle their laughter when the porcelain beast spit water, gargled and swallowed—ending with a gurgling, satisfied . . . belch.

✦ ✦ ✦

Although she enjoyed both the social life and the large tips handed to her so casually by the soldiers when she moonlighted each evening as a cocktail waitress, it was Tammy's day job that challenged and fulfilled her, giving her a strong measure of personal satisfaction and growth. With both her skills and her English ripening, she positioned herself as a secretary at the NCO Club. Put in charge of bookkeeping and accounting, she shouldered new responsibilities with ease.

More importantly, she discovered that the business of numbers was a universal language—and she was fluent in it.

The same aptitude for the mathematics she had once traded in school for food now provided her with a higher level of income on the military base, which translated to even more money for the eleven brothers and sisters at home. Money that kept food in their bellies. Money that purchased better quality clothing. Money that eased Má's work hours at the market. Enough money, in fact, that her family could move a few blocks away, from their one-room hut with its dirt floor into three rooms built on concrete, upgrading from coconut-leaf thatch to a tiled roof.

Last Sunday, Tammy took her weekly bus trip down National Highway 1 for the hour ride home. Relieved to be out of the gated compound, she invited Vui on a small shopping spree. A blouse and sandals for this sister nearest her in age, a stylish mini skirt for herself. Tea and dessert in downtown Sài Gòn.

"So much money! Should we spend it so?" Vui wondered.

Tammy grinned at her sister's doubtful face. "Remember what Ba always says? '*In order to give, you must have; you can't give if you don't have.*'" She paused. "I *have*, Sister Three." A gentle firmness seeped into her voice. "I have—so, I *give*."

✦ ✦ ✦

Clank. Clank.

Tammy poured a tumble of coins into the counting machine and turned to the table where piles of change waited to be rolled. Fifty dimes per roll. Forty quarters. Fifty nickels. She shook her head at the mounds and mounds of well-earned money that bored soldiers dropped into the slot machines—hoping for a win, shrugging at the losses—whiling away the hours between field maneuvers. More than fifty thousand troops rippled in and out of the base, leaving a wake of office work and accounting behind them.

They'll feel no judgment from me. She shrugged. *Besides, all their spending provides me with a good-paying job.*

And, oh, what a job. In spite of meticulous bookkeeping on her part, the vastness of the club's business—the men consumed huge quantities of food and alcohol—made keeping track of inventory a constant challenge.

"We're due for an inspection, Tammy," Sergeant Leon had told her yesterday. "I got word they're gonna inventory the liquor and the food. The auditors'll be here at 0900."

"How minh-ee?"

"Two. You take one, I'll take one." He gave her a slow wink. "You'll take care a-things?"

She liked this jovial boss with the kind heart and gave him a shy smile of agreement. A well-run club was a good reflection on him. And her. She would see to everything.

Tammy glanced at the wall clock. The auditors were due to arrive at any minute.

She slid the narrow scarf from her hair, pulled a comb through the silky strands and retied the flirty red wisp. She scooted through the door and down the hall to the supply room.

She had a record to maintain; her club always received good marks from inspectors, no small achievement if a person took into account the amount of spillage and over-pour that occurred naturally when liquor was sold by the drink. Not to mention the potential for making incorrect change and coming up short.

Forty shots in a bottle.

Twenty-five cents for each shot.

Now, where did that missing five dollars go?

Hadn't she driven herself crazy trying to account for every cent, balance all the books and make everything perfect for Sergeant Leon?

Oh, she understood the U.S. government's demand for accountability. The taverns on base served thousands of men, hundreds of thirsty customers each night going through cases of inventory. Bourbon. Scotch. The auditors simply wanted to be certain none of it ended up on the black market.

But, perfection? Impossible.

Tammy took a deep breath, knowing she held the upper hand. There had been other inspectors, other minor errors in the books. She had her own technique to protect Sergeant Leon's job, a technique she had mastered. Determined to cover for any small discrepancies that might reflect poorly on her boss, she smoothed her white blouse into the skirt that circled her slender waist and stepped into the supply room.

One of the auditors whistled, low and long, through his teeth and elbowed the other fellow. Tammy pretended not to hear. Or see.

"Well, hello-oo *there*," he drawled.

The younger man's eyebrows shot up. He started to say something, stopped, blushed. Just then, Sergeant Leon stuck his head inside the door.

"One-a you gentlemen here to inspect food?" He beckoned. "Folla me."

The first soldier glanced at Tammy, nodded regretfully and traipsed after Sergeant Leon.

Tammy smiled slightly at the young auditor and lowered her gaze. She tilted her head a bit and looked up, secretly confident. "You red-hee do in-speh-shun?"

"Sure, Hon . . . er . . ." His eyes lingered on the nametag she had pinned over her left breast. His gaze skittered across her chest before coming to settle on her face. He blushed. "Sure . . . uh . . . T-Tammy."

She turned to the storage shelves to hide the grin that teased the corners of her mouth. Her arm swept wide, indicating an ample reservoir of liquor ready, waiting to be inventoried.

They both knew the routine: Count the full cases. Count the partial cases. Check the totals against the paperwork she had sent in.

They both knew the details involved: Count the opened bottles. Weigh each on the scale to determine how many ounces were left. Convert those ounces to shots sold. Determine how much money should have been reported. Check the totals against the paperwork she had sent in.

"You lie Tah-mee coun lik-ker?" she offered eagerly, dragging a step stool next to the long wooden shelves. "You lie Tah-mee clamb laud-der?"

The young man looked away, suddenly self conscious. "S-sure. F-fine. You climb the ladder."

Tammy stepped upward, cautiously aware of the high-heeled sandals she fancied as an extension to make her bare legs look longer under her new black mini skirt.

With studied deliberation, she stretched to reach and tally the liquor inventory for him. She counted the full cases. She counted the partial cases. From the top of her perch, she allowed him time—plenty of time—to check the numbers she gave him against the paperwork she had sent in.

"Looks like everything is in order." The relief in his voice was evident. "Climb down now and let's work on those lower rows of opened bottles."

Ignoring his suggestion, Tammy stooped over slightly and in halting, but even tones, began counting in English. She knew she could fudge a bit; the man would accept the totals she gave, never even seeing the few bottles she was juggling to the back row that, otherwise, would skew her bookwork. He was too busy admiring her legs.

With studious attention and as worldly a look as she could muster, she gave him her count and caught him staring. His boyish face turned the color of ripe watermelon, deep crimson and nearly as wholesome. Tammy ignored the slight twinge of guilt tugging at her conscience the way a persistent toddler pulled at Má's hand.

Bending toward the next shelf, she twisted her torso just far enough to inch her skirt a notch higher. From the corner of her eye, she saw the young man tighten his grip on the clipboard to steady it. Impossible as it seemed, his face was redder yet.

She had done the calculations; she knew exactly which bottles she would hand him to be weighed and accounted for. And she knew, without a doubt, that the totals would match the paperwork she had sent in for Sergeant Leon.

Of that, she was certain.

Even in war, boys are boys and men are men, she smirked. *No matter which nation's uniform they wear.*

CHAPTER 12

Dormitory, 1972
Long Bình, Việt Nam

Testing the Waters

Tammy stretched out on top of her mattress, luxuriating in the rare silence of the room. At this hour of the day, most of her friends were still at work. In a few minutes she, too, would be at work, this time at her evening job. She studied the springs of Hoa's bunk overhead, deep in thought.

Her eyes widened.

In one fluid movement, she rolled to her stomach and slid the journal from its nest under the pillow. Propping herself on her elbows, Tammy turned to a blank page, pressing the book's cover until it lay flat.

Unlike yesterday's stumbling attempts, this afternoon the words rippled, rushed, then streamed onto the paper. Nearly drowning in the current, she held her breath, afraid to disrupt the lines flowing in the wake of her pencil.

Finished at last, she paused to read what she had written.

Love Dissolved

I.

A man
Walking on a road
Meets a woman.
They get to know each other,
Both struck by Fate
That bright sunny day
To love.
Love swells
From the words of their lips,
Their smiles and laughter.
They love each other.

II.

She is heartbroken
One day when
He leaves.
Winds blow from the battlefield
With news
He has fallen.
She weeps for her loss.
And one day
On the old road,
A woman
Wears a death veil on her head.
She trots slowly

Behind the coffin
Of her lover.
She knows of life and love.
Now she knows of loss.

With a graceful spiral of her wrist, Tammy signed her name in willowy letters and tucked the pencil tenderly into the valley of the spine to mark the page. Her open palm lingered over the words, hovering as though warmth radiated from them. At last, she closed her journal with a romantic sigh and slipped it under the pillow.

Poems spoke to her soul; they fed her spirit. They seeped into her being, whether she was writing them or whether she was pouring over the words, tender and profound, of others. And, lately, she surprised herself by filling her diary, scrawling rivers of poetry whenever she had a few free minutes or a quiet moment alone.

Alone?

Tammy jumped from her bunk in alarm.

Shouldn't her ride to work be here by now?

Racing down the stairs and out the door, she scanned the street in both directions. The late-afternoon heat, as heavy as buckets of water and just as wet, settled on her shoulders. The air was thick enough to spread on a baguette. The compound was busy, but she saw no sign of her friends.

"Fortune certainly isn't smiling on me today," she huffed. How long should she wait? Or, what if they had already come and she—with head and heart awash in her journal—had missed them?

It's only a 15-minute walk, if I hurry, she decided.

She considered the open toes of her sandals and the height of the heels. She glared at the softness of the sun-baked asphalt. She frowned at a street still void of her friends.

Well, if I don't leave now, I'll be late.

Squinting into the harsh sunlight, Tammy tottered down the road as fast as her shoes would let her. Before sweat could bead her brow, an army truck slowed, swerved close to her and stopped. A uniformed GI sat in the passenger seat, his cocked elbow resting on the edge of the open window.

"Where-ya headed?" he hollered as the truck idled.

She raised her voice over the engine's rumble. "The May NCO."

"All the way to the Main NCO? It's still awful hot out for a walk that far." He conferred with the driver and turned back again. "We can give you a ride. You want-a lift?"

"Shure!"

The door swung open and the soldier hopped down.

Tammy noticed his fair skin, slight build and the clean-cut, American look of him. He didn't tower over her like most American men. As she climbed high into the truck, their eyes met.

Not blue. Not green. Not brown. She dared a second look. *Hazel,* she decided.

He slid in, settled beside her and shut the door. "I'm Paul." His thumb jerked to indicate the driver. "And this's my buddy, John."

John? Truly, yet another John? Tammy replaced the laughter that bubbled inside her with a wide grin and greeted him.

"He-llo, John." She swiveled her head to face the first GI. "He-llo, Paw."

"And you're . . ." he prompted.

"Tah-mee. My nam ih Tah-mee." With the ends of her fingers, she flipped strands of her thick hair over her shoulder and smiled at him through her lashes.

Like so many soldiers she had met, these two were jovial, easy to talk to. She knew by his insignia that Paul's rank was SP4. "Wha wor you do?"

"I'm a mechanic. John'n me both repair Army vehicles, like this truck we're in. We keep 'em in tip-top condition. What-a bout you, Tammy? What-a you do at the club?"

"I boo-keep by day. Nigh time, I caw-tay wait-reh."

"Oh yeah? You a cocktail waitress there, too?" John piped in. "Then you must know Hoa."

"Shure. Hoa my beh frien. She my cuh-zin."

Paul leaned closer, close enough that she noticed his dark wavy hair. He nudged her side with his elbow. "Just between you and me, John's got-a crush on that cousin of yours." Speaking out the corner of his mouth, he raised his voice loud enough for his buddy to hear. "John thinks Hoa's awfully cute."

"Yabetchurbottomdollar I think she's cute!" John downshifted, slowed and pulled up to the club. "More than cute." Lowering one hand to the seat between them, he swiveled to face Tammy. "Hoa is beautiful." His voice deepened. "Really beautiful."

Tammy agreed. Her pretty cousin caught and held the attention of nearly every man she met. Lively, fun and funny, Hoa was just as popular with her coworkers on base as she was with the soldiers. She made friends without effort. Not only did Tammy share a bunk with her at the dorm, the two cousins also spent their free time together.

"You know she wor here?" Tammy indicated the club with a tilt of her head.

"Oh, yeah, I know Hoa works here." John's teeth caught his lower lip. He looked sideways at her. "You think she'd go out with me?"

"You go see, fine ow. Go in-sigh," Tammy urged. "Go in-sigh. Taw wih her. You go see."

"Maybe I will." John winked and revved the engine. "Talking with Hoa is just what I'm hoping to do."

Extending her thanks for the ride, Tammy mentioned she really needed to get to work. Paul sprang from the truck and, with a sweeping flourish, extended a warm hand to help her clamber out.

Was it her imagination, or did he really hold it longer than necessary? She smiled shyly and hurried inside.

"I'll see-ya later," Paul called after her.

Her heart skipped a beat.

Will he? she wondered. *Will he really?*

Although the men lumbered off in the truck to finish their own shifts, John did show up at the club that night. Alone. And it was obvious he was not there for the food or drink.

From across the room, she watched Hoa and John flirt, admiring the way her cousin tossed her head back in full-throated laughter, exposing the long, smooth skin of her neck. She noted how the two made opportunities to touch each other. Often. Hoa's hand on his shirtsleeve, John's fingers lingering when he accepted the drink she offered. Tammy saw the way their heads bent close together over the table.

Were they whispering, maybe sharing a secret? Did he just steal a kiss?

John and Hoa smiled deeply into each other's eyes, as though no one else mattered and not another soul was in the room. They acted like the world existed for them alone.

Tammy felt her heart catch and stumble at the tender sight.

Because she was doing some bartending as well as waitressing, she was not as available to mingle with the customers as Hoa was. However, when her workload slowed, Tammy joined her spirited cousin and found herself laughing, teasing and making conversation with both Hoa and John.

Too bad there's no one around to be impressed with my clever comments tonight, she thought. Regretfully, Tammy went back to her post, tending bar and seeing to the customers.

But all evening long, she kept a wistful eye on the door, wishing Paul would walk in.

CHAPTER 13

Lê Lợi Street, 1973
Sài Gòn, Việt Nam

Pulled Apart

Hoa puffed at the cloud of steam hovering over her cup. "Have you heard from your GI lately?"

"Hmmm." The clatter in the coffee house nearly drowned Tammy's answer.

"Is that a yes or a no?"

Staring through her cousin like a soldier suffering shell shock, Tammy slouched over the round table. One elbow rested on the top to support the defeated chin propped on the heel of her cupped palm.

Hoa snapped her fingers in front of Tammy's nose. "Did you even hear what I asked you?"

"What?" Tammy started. She straightened in her chair. "Oh, I'm sorry. I guess I was daydreaming again."

"I wondered if you've gotten any letters lately."

"You mean from Paul?"

"Of course I mean from Paul. Who else would be writing you letters?"

Tammy's breath caught; she looked away.

Hoa tapped her temple with one finger. "Where is your mind today, Sister Two?"

Tammy knew exactly where her mind was. Everywhere. Scattered to the ends of the earth.

Here was the one friend who would understand, really understand her feelings, yet Tammy couldn't bring herself to expose the misery consuming every waking moment and, truthfully, consuming many of the hours when she should be sleeping.

Yes, she had heard from Paul. Wasn't that the one bright spot in her otherwise miserable life?

Paul's letters arrived with the steadfast predictability of the rice harvest. When the Army had shipped him back to the States several months ago, he promised he would write. She looked forward to each envelope, knowing it would tell her more about his life at a military base called Fort Meade. She liked hearing about his friends Ken and Joyce, the holidays they celebrated and the things they did together. The minute, day-to-day details had the familiarity of the military she knew so well, seasoned with a foreign spice that whetted her appetite and heightened her curiosity about America.

Although it was excruciatingly painful to write him with her limited English, Tammy responded frequently, from her bunk during the stillness of night or from her desk at the Main NCO when she had some free time. She kept a bilingual dictionary at hand to muddle through the writing and the reading.

"Well? Are you going to tell me?"

Tammy heard the impatience in Hoa's voice and realized she still hadn't answered her question.

"Another letter came yesterday."

"And?"

"And he said that he hopes to see me again."

Her friend's eyes crinkled at the corners before a pleased smile lit her face. "See! I told you distance means nothing when there is love."

Tammy tensed slightly.

"Sister Two? What's wrong?"

What *was* wrong with her?

Tammy sorted through the complicated knot her life had become, trying to separate the distinct threads.

To start with, Paul was thousands of miles away—and she was here. Alone. Alone and missing him and missing the fun times the two of them shared with John and Hoa. The foursome had struck a close friendship and spent many happy hours together on base, mostly casual times. Walking, talking, eating and drinking, laughing and teasing and flirting.

But that had all ended, ended too soon, hadn't it? Gone in a blink of fast farewells when the American government began pulling back, thinning the troops and emptying the bases last year in preparation for handing over the war—and the heavy equipment they would leave behind—to the South Vietnamese government.

She tugged at another loop in her snarled life: her absent friends.

One by one, they had left Long Bình, the GIs she grew up with during the five years she worked and lived at the base. The young men who, like her, had sacrificed their youth at the altar of war. Gone were the soldiers who shared funny stories, sly winks, dirty jokes and photographs of their girlfriends, their mothers, their children, their motorcyles and their dogs. Gone were the warriors who cried in their beers over the atrocities of battle, instigated a brawl over an insignificant cigarette and handed candy and gum to every street urchin who crossed their path.

One after another, the war-weary troops had boarded a Freedom Bird for home.

Hoa interrupted her friend's reverie. "You're impossible today."

Tammy shook her head, disgusted with herself. "You're right. I'm . . . lost, I guess. I-I wish I could be better company for you. Please forgive me."

"Well, I'm expected at home, anyway." Hoa stood. "So I'll leave you with your daydreams. See you tomorrow?"

Waving a half-hearted goodbye, Tammy nodded absently, already deep in thought again.

When their jobs dissolved, her Vietnamese coworkers had left the compound, too, returning to their villages or seeking fresh starts in the Philippines, Thailand, Cambodia or the United States. Many moved to Sài Gòn, joining the thousands of displaced civilian support-staff from the other military bases who were also hoping to find some kind of work.

Ah, work. Her prized job.

As the military withdrew, Long Bình had become a body without a spirit. Empty buildings, dusty barracks, deserted streets. A skeleton staff was all that remained where tens of thousands of people once bustled.

With her elevated position in Restaurant and Food Services, Tammy was one of the last civilians at the base. Like the wagon trains in the American westerns she had seen, Jeeps, tanks and trucks left trails of dust as convoy after convoy wound out the gates. Near the end of the year, only the military police remained.

Casting a lingering glance over her shoulder, Tammy had boarded a bus back to Khánh Hội.

By January, she was ensconced at a desk in the middle of Sài Gòn. It was a twenty-minute ride from her parents' home to the tall corporate building the Army occupied on the tree-lined boulevard. She passed the American Embassy and the lush gardens of the Temple on her way to work each day. Ba, who worked a second job in the area, often sought her company to stroll the city streets or sit at a café over cognac to discuss war and politics. She found it easy to confide her fears and hopes, to admit her dreams of an education and a better life for them all. Ba, deep-thinking and insightful, listened intently to his favored first child.

While the military decided what to leave behind and what to ship to the States, Tammy helped her boss process the massive mounds of paperwork. She filed and shredded, packed and boxed until, by early March, she, too, found herself numbered among Sài Gòn's unemployed. In the end, the American flag was furled at a ceremony marking the official deactivation of the Military Assistance Command-Vietnam (MAC-V).

Deciding she had occupied the café table long enough, Tammy shoved aside her cold coffee and grabbed the paperback she had brought along. *Maybe I'll read in the park for an hour or two,* she decided.

She strolled down Lê Lợi Street, in the heart of the traditional French Quarter, past posh hotels. She poked through the wares offered at small stalls, peered inside the large bookstore, drooled at the ice cream shop. She turned at an intersection and wandered until she came to a Temple where she sought a patch of dappled shade on the grounds.

Sinking to the lush grass under a coconut tree, she closed her eyes, feeling the sun's warm palm on her back, and ignored the James Bond paperback in her lap. She had spent hours and hours reading over the past several months, reading everything she could get her hands on. Trashy novels, light romances, mysteries and suspense. James Bond thrillers.

Escape, she realized. *I read to escape reality. I have no life of my own, so I lose myself in the adventures of fictional people.*

She picked again at her tangled past.

Returning home was like trying to squeeze into an *Áo dài* she'd outgrown. She had tried on her old life, her old friends, her old haunts—even her old sleeping mat at her parents' house. None of it fit anymore.

Conversations with so many of her neighborhood girlfriends felt vague and empty. Her world had revolved around the military, real life-and-death drama and a cast of characters totally alien to her friends. By contrast, their interests seemed vain and frivolous. Their relationships dwindled to the superficial.

Reluctant to reduce herself to sewing (horrors!), hauling water or selling fish in the market, Tammy had not yet found a job that utilized her honed skills and her knowledge of a foreign language. No job could compete with the paycheck and tips she was accustomed to.

Unfortunately, as her savings shrank, her family felt the financial strain. Gone were the small extras, shopping trips to the city, new clothes. Stoic, Má—whose belly swelled with baby thirteen—went to the market every day, working longer and longer hours.

"You could join me there, Thuận," Má suggested.

"No." Tammy didn't mean for her answer to sound so clipped, but the idea was unthinkable.

"Twice the selling, twice the *dong*," Má wheedled.

"My time is better spent earning higher wages."

"Higher wages?" Her eyebrows shot up.

"My time is better spent earning higher wages," Tammy repeated, more firmly this time.

"But, Daughter Two, you're not bringing in higher . . ." Má's mouth clamped closed. She turned away with shuttered eyes.

When Vui—Sister Three—lengthened her day by several hours helping Má at the marketplace, Tammy tried not to let guilt consume her. But it was hard to watch this favorite sister working such long hours. Tammy cast her net even wider, fishing for a suitable job.

I should have boxed my bookkeeping skills with all those papers and shipped them to America where they might be of some use, she grumbled.

Being home among her sisters and brothers made her squirm and yearn for freedom.

A tiger needs the forest. A fish needs the sea. And I need . . . What?

What, exactly, did she need? Why did she feel so displaced, so incomplete, so unfulfilled—even among those she loved? For years, she had visited her family every Sunday for a few hours of chatting, eating and shopping, bringing *dong* to Má. But it seemed they had all grown apart. *Or, perhaps I'm the one who did the growing?*

Her family's habits and routines and customs were no longer hers; her Americanized ideas and language and concepts did not match theirs. *I feel like a Vietnamese girl without a culture.* She frowned. *At times, I'm not certain I even feel Vietnamese.*

Surprised at the accuracy of her unflinching self assessment, Tammy heaved a sigh of acknowledgement.

Which left the final kink in her knotted life.

The other man she loved.

Khai.

CHAPTER 14

Vietnamese Command Post, 1973
Cần Thơ, Việt Nam

Touching Reality

Tammy stared out the open window of the small bus. The canal-laced countryside of the Mekong Delta fascinated her with its mangrove swamps and low-lying marshes. Craning her neck to ogle a stilt house, its skinny legs stuck in the river like a plump woman wading with her skirts hitched high, Tammy didn't even attempt to smother a fit of giggles.

The 170 kilometer ride to Cần Thơ was a revelation. After the rush and confusion of city life, these verdant vistas soothed her eyes and calmed her spirit. She had never really been outside Sài Gòn before, other than those weekly trips back and forth to her job at Long Bình, of course.

But even a city girl can appreciate a scene like this! Tammy's head pivoted from side to side as her eager eyes took in every detail.

Tiny bamboo huts squatted behind wide rice fields dotted with peasants working the paddies: men, women and children dressed in Áo bà ba—traditional black-silk pajamas—and woven hats to shade their eyes from the piercing sun. Here and there, lumbering water buffalo grazed. In the distance, the fronds of coconut trees feathered the blue, blue sky.

Lulled by the peaceful setting, the rocking bus and the midday heat, Tammy felt the urge to nap. All it took, however, was a wayward thought about Khai to make her eyes fly open, her heart flutter and her mouth go dry.

Khai.

Handsome, lean and fit, the dashing lieutenant in the South Vietnamese Army was the object of her respect as well as more than a few of her romantic notions.

When his latest letter arrived with an invitation to visit him at his command post outside of Cần Thơ, Tammy knew she needed to go. It had already been several weeks since he was in Khánh Hội on leave. She needed to see him again. To talk with him. To confide in him. To tell him . . .

The bus lurched to a stop.

She could see Khai in his khaki-green uniform, leaning against a wall at the corner, waiting, waiting for her.

After a formal bow of greeting, he reached for the small bag she carried. "You must be hungry."

"Y-yes," she stuttered. "I-I didn't think to bring food with me on the bus."

Silly girl, she chided herself for her awkwardness. This was Khai, after all, the older brother of one of her friends. The man who put her at her ease, who made her feel comfortable. Hadn't they both marveled at the instant connection they felt?

"Would you like to go somewhere to eat?" Khai's smile was as inviting as his question.

They walked across the street to order lemongrass soup at a shady outdoor café. By the time their meal arrived, they were laughing and talking with the effortlessness of two people who had acquaintances in common and a mutual history to discuss. The five-year age difference that seemed insurmountable when they were children meant nothing since they had become reacquainted a few months earlier.

As they lingered over coffee, Khai laid out his plans for her overnight stay. "I thought we would start with a leisurely ride through the countryside. Does that appeal to you?"

Tammy nodded, her eyes brightening at the prospect.

Khai tied her bag to the handle bars of his Honda. Throwing one long leg over the seat, he steadied the motorcycle while Tammy edged her right hip onto the pillion and curved an arm around his waist. With her left hand, she adjusted the long, straight skirt of her white *Áo dài*, gripping the edge of the seat when his booted foot jumped on the kick starter. He revved the throttle, eased out on the clutch and turned with smooth finesse into the street.

Perched sidesaddle, she clung to the seat and Khai.

He drove them down dirt roads so narrow they were passable only by motorcycle, bicycle or foot. Occasionally, he would point out something of interest. A sugarcane grove over there. A young boy riding a water buffalo over here. Someone washing clothes in a canal.

"And, look," Khai shouted over the motor. "See that house?" He pointed to a hut with a tin roof. "That house belongs to the friends I mentioned. They want to meet you before you leave."

Her streaming hair tickling the wind, Tammy cast dreamy eyes on the bucolic scenery. "It's hard to believe we're in the middle of a war."

"What did you say?"

As she leaned closer to repeat her comment in his ear, Tammy snugged her arm around Khai's waist. In contrast to American GIs who were so free with their hugs and kisses, tossing their arms casually around the shoulders of a date or pulling a girl boldly into their laps, her cultural mores limited physical contact in public and, secretly, she was grateful for the clandestine opportunity now to touch him.

Perhaps Khai, too, feels the thrill?

She grinned at the back of his bare head where neatly cropped black hair brushed the edge of his shirt collar.

Khai's small command post, with its dirt roads and crude buildings, paled in comparison to Long Bình and MAC-V. He walked her past the handful of tents to a three-sided hut with coconut-leaf walls atop a dirt floor and pointed through the doorless opening.

"You'll sleep here, in the women's quarters."

She scratched a fresh bite on her elbow, knowing she would be grateful that night for the mosquito netting she saw over each cot.

By the time the evening was over, Tammy had met his friends and fellow officers. Khai took pride in the introductions, quick to point out Tammy's talents, praising her abilities, job skills and goals. His obvious admiration made her glow.

In the quiet of late night, they sat under a sliver of moon whose reflection rippled across puddles in the dirt, a spotlight to dancing moths. The couple's soft murmurs were a counter-melody to a chorus of crickets as the subtle heartbeat of rural life pulsed around them, its cool breath brushing their skin, toying with their hair.

"Look up, Thuận. I wanted you to see the sky out here."

Together, they admired the winking stars, embroidered in sparkling clusters and shiny trails that swept across the clear heavens everywhere they looked. Over, behind, around them and beyond.

I can reach out and touch one, Tammy thought. But she knew it wasn't true. Like so many things in her life, they were beyond her reach.

Khai's comments shifted to the war and politics. To America's withdrawal from the country. That was one of the things that drew her to him, his deep thoughts and his willingness to discuss them with her. Like Ba, Khai was an intellectual and Tammy found that both men respected her opinions.

"From my perspective, the South is facing serious trouble. I see this war escalating and not in our favor. What do you think, Thuận?"

Her response was slow, thoughtful. "Truthfully, the same as you. With backing from Russia, the North Vietnamese will surely overthrow our government. We don't stand a chance without the support of America. I felt such a sense of desolation when they all left." She also felt fear, deep down and heavy, knowing that her presence in the country threatened her family's safety. The North had a long memory and a longer arm; her relationship with the U.S. military wasn't a secret.

Her eyes searched his, noticing how the moonlight caressed his high cheekbones.

"In fact, that's why I accepted your invitation to visit." She paused. "I-I need to tell you something."

Even in the dim light, she could see a muscle in his jaw twitch at her tone.

When he didn't respond, she continued. "I . . . well . . . I-I've decided to leave Việt Nam."

"Leave? Why? Where? What are you saying?"

Tammy placed gentle fingers over his lips. "Shhh. Give me a chance to explain."

After a long silence, she whispered, "There's someone I haven't told you about. An American soldier. A man I was seeing before, well, before—you. He was shipped back to the States months ago and, and . . ."

"He wants you, too," he said flatly.

"T-too?"

"Don't you know, Thuận? Haven't you felt it? Can't you see?" Khai leaned toward her with an unexpected urgency in his brown eyes. He reached for her hand. "I find myself falling in love with you."

His declaration of love startled Tammy. Startled her, yet didn't surprise her. Not really. Hadn't she sensed this from his last few letters? Hadn't she felt something, some *thing* deep within herself, reaching out, connecting the two of them?

Undeniably, they shared a deep bond.

Like her, Khai was a Big Dreamer, a thoughtful fellow who believed that education breeds success. A man with High Hopes, hopes for himself, hopes for his future, hopes for the future of his country. He planted his feet on the same plane as hers. It was, she knew, part of their mutual attraction.

And there was no denying Khai was a catch. A romantic older man in uniform, an exceptionally good-looking, clean-cut, officer-with-a-future, the kind of fellow every Vietnamese girl hoped to marry.

But that was the snag. She wasn't Vietnamese, not anymore. She didn't belong here.

She gazed with yearning at the man beside her.

Paul.

Remember Paul.

Her nagging conscience forced her to sit up straighter, to ease away from Khai. He clutched her hand more firmly, pulling her back toward him.

"Thuận?"

"Paul asked me, Khai. In his last letter, he asked me." She gulped. "He asked me, and I answered."

"You accepted."

"I accepted."

"When?"

"When? What do you mean?"

"When do you leave?" His voice was hollow.

"Next week."

Silence pressed against them. Solid. Tangible. Hushing the crickets. Distilling the night into this one, important moment.

"There's no changing your mind?"

Quickly, to deny temptation, she shook her head.

Khai placed the weight of his strong hands on her shoulders. He looked deep into her eyes, eyes with pools spilling diamonds that trickled down her cheeks.

"Although I understand, I wish you wouldn't leave, Thuận. But I'm not going to ask you to stay. I love you enough to let you go."

His hands slid up the sides of her neck to cup her smooth face. One thumb brushed a tear from her chin. "If Fate decides we should be in each other's life, I'll find you. No matter what, I'll find you."

His own eyes glistened, the puddled moisture reflecting pinpoints from the stars overhead.

"Remember, Thuận, I found you once in this life. I'll search until I find you again."

A solitary cloud scuttered across the sky to shroud the moon.

CHAPTER 15

Airports, October 22, 1973
From Việt Nam to the United States of America

Rough Landing

A bank of thick clouds obliterated the ground below her. In the snap of a finger, her country disappeared.

Tammy had hoped to experience vantage views of water birds that scalloped the skies over Sài Gòn on this, her first plane ride. Ông Thầy once told his students Việt Nam was shaped like a bent bamboo shoulder-pole with heavy rice baskets on each end. He said the Sài Gòn River spread itself across the landscape like a many-clawed dragon. She only regretted that the clouds kept her from seeing these wonders for herself.

Her flight to America had left early that morning, while Sài Gòn only stirred and stretched. After the paperwork and one-way ticket arrived from Paul a few months earlier, she began her preparations to meet his family in St. Louis,

Missouri. Paul wrote that he had a thirty-day leave and would fly from Fort Meade to join them. It hadn't taken long to get her shots and x-rays and complete the process necessary for a visa. Nor had it taken much time to tie up the loose threads of her life.

Like a dying person bequeathing her earthly possessions, Tammy distributed the extra clothes, shoes, jewelry and odds and ends she had amassed during her years at Long Bình among her sisters and girlfriends. Packing her nicest *Áo dàis*, she filled the rest of the small suitcase with her journals and a few more clothes. She gave the last of her savings to Má. The family needed it more than she did. The remaining *dong* she exchanged for American dollars—ten dollars—plenty, she figured, to get by until she was settled in the States.

A parade of friends, neighbors and family members had accompanied her onto the tarmac at Tân Sơn Nhứt Airfield. They all stood around chattering in a cluster of mopeds, bicycles and cyclos.

After a flurry of well wishing and lingering farewells from those she loved so dearly, Tammy reached for Sister Three.

"Goodbye, Vui," she choked, stepping back from their long embrace. "I'll miss you."

Má edged closer, her fingers laced primly at her waist, until she was beside the two of them. "Goodbye *con*—my child. Remember us. Remember home. Remember where you came from." She looked deeply into her daughter's eyes as though probing her soul. "May Fortune smile on you at last."

Tammy thanked Má and turned to her father.

"Ba, I . . ."

He gazed at his eldest daughter, the attractive child whose softly rounded cheeks mirrored his own. Enfolding her in his lanky arms, Ba cradled her head against his chest just as he had when she was a little girl. "Thuận?"

She clung a minute longer before leaning back to meet his gaze. "Yes, Ba?"

"Remember, *con*, your name is your only possession of real value. See that you honor it."

She bowed her head, aware of the catch in her throat. "I will, Ba. I will."

As the tangerine sun rose higher on the horizon, her tiny suitcase was stowed safely in the plane's underbelly and Tammy boarded. From the top of the metal stairs, she turned for one last, lingering look. Tears coursing down her face, she stepped into the stomach of the PanAm jet, her own Freedom Bird, a scared little girl clinging to everything she owned in the world: a fifth-grade education, ten dollars and a dream.

A scant three hours later, when they landed at the Manila Airport, Tammy rushed to purchase postcards and stamps with a bit of her money. She scrawled a quick note to her family to let them know she had survived the first leg of her journey and actually set foot in the Philippines; she would write later to give her new mailing address.

A night sky greeted her in Honolulu. While the crew refueled, she reclaimed her luggage and followed a line through Customs. Not until then did she understand that this beautiful place was part of America.

If Hawaii looks like this, St. Louis must be a tropical paradise, she thought to herself as she walked around the tastefully decorated airport. Tân Sơn Nhứt was coarse, primitive in comparison.

The third time the plane landed, Tammy exited in a daze. Oddly, even after so many hours in the air, it was still night time—although the harsh glare of bright lights and the noisy commotion at the airport made her entertain the idea that no one slept in this place called San Francisco.

Confused at the crackling instructions over the loud speaker, Tammy stopped an airport attendant and showed her the ticket.

"Where to I go?"

The attendant pointed. "That way."

Tammy located her seat on the plane and promptly fell asleep. At the fourth stop, she stumbled around the strange airport, re-boarded and closed her eyes again.

The next thing she knew, it was daylight. She had arrived!

Tammy followed the other passengers off the plane to claim her suitcase. Pulling out the small address book in her purse, she found the phone number Paul had given her, got directions to a telephone booth and blundered through her first collect call.

"I heer," she told Paul's sister.

"Good," said a voice at the other end. "Do you have the pictures my brother sent so you'll recognize us?"

"Yes."

"Stay near the door and watch for us. We'll be there in about an hour."

"Fine. I see you den."

With time to spare, Tammy located a restroom to brush her teeth and freshen up. From there, she obediently stationed herself just inside the doorway of the airport.

She stood, holding her small suitcase.

She watched people coming in and going out.

She saw people hugging goodbye and kissing hello.

She watched people step onto a . . . a . . . a *moving* staircase . . . and disappear from sight at the top. Tammy stared, fascinated. It had no beginning; it had no end. And, apparently, it went nowhere. She would be afraid to stand on it; she feared she might fall off.

When no one showed up to collect her, Tammy left her post at the door just long enough to place another call.

"They already left for the airport to get you," said someone at other end of the phone.

"Buh dey not heer."

"Yes, but they will be. Go back to the door. Stay there so they can find you."

Tammy hurried to her lookout, clutching the black-and-white pictures Paul had sent, staring into each passing face, anxiously comparing the photographs against every female who walked by. Truthfully, she hadn't met many American women at Long Binh and here, on foreign soil, she couldn't tell one from another.

They all look alike! Remembering Captain John's confusion when he spouted those same words, she nearly laughed out loud.

After two more hours had passed, Tammy flagged down a harried luggage handler. She indicated the entry in her address book.

"How far thih place?"

He barely glanced where she pointed. "Not far."

"Tha wha dey tell me. Buh no one heer."

He shrugged. "Just wait."

This time, she sat on the edge of her suitcase. What if they hadn't been able to find her?

But, how could they not find me? She was a petite, black-haired Vietnamese woman in a land of giants. Wearing a turquoise *Áo dài* in a sea of polyester pantsuits, faded Levis and flashy mini skirts. *They must know I look different,* she thought.

Her stomach growled, reminding her it was now early afternoon.

She placed another call.

"They're there, Tammy. They're at the airport, looking for you."

"I am heer, too. I loo-keen for dem. How dey mith me?"

Panicked, she couldn't voice the question gnawing at her gut: Had Paul changed his mind?

What if he didn't want her here, after all?

Was this a cruel joke of some kind?

She was scared, really scared; her chest ached from the fierce pounding of her heart. She shoved her fingers through the crown of her hair, trying hard to think. She couldn't call Paul; she didn't have his phone number. Besides, he was in Fort Meade, Maryland. The few dollars and loose change in her purse wouldn't go far, if the airport café signs were any indication. What could she do? It was already 4:00 p.m. She paced at the foot of the moving stairs and finally planted herself near the doorway again.

"Something I can help you with, Miss?" asked a deep voice behind her.

Tammy swiveled around and looked up and up, into the warm eyes of the biggest black man she'd ever seen.

"Yes, yes!" Tammy grabbed his uniformed arm. "I bean way-teen."

"How long?"

"Since sev-tirty thih more-neen."

He whistled between his teeth, long and low.

"See?" She showed him the Polaroids and pointed to the address in her book. "One how-er, dey say. One how-er!"

He read the entry and looked at her. "Hmmm. Do you still have your ticket?"

Tammy riffled through her paperwork, her visa and her passport, until she found the ticket. He thumbed through its pages.

"Mind if I take this?"

She shook her head.

"Now, you stay here and I'll be right back. You understand?"

Tammy nodded. *Where else would I go?* The irony of his instructions wasn't lost on her, but, for the first time all day, she felt a glimmer of hope.

Ten minutes later, the man returned, gesturing. "Follow me."

By then, Tammy would have gone with anybody who would take her. She followed him. As far as the moving stairs. With only a hint of hesitancy, she took a deep breath and lurched onto the first step, surprised when nothing bad happened. Her exit at the top went smoother.

I just scaled my first American mountain! She felt smug at the idea.

The man led her to the TWA ticket counter where, stretching the cord to its full length, a female clerk handed her a telephone receiver and smiled warmly.

"Someone wants to talk to you."

"Me?" Tammy looked at the black porter and back to the woman. "You shure me?"

"Yes, you."

Tammy held the phone to her ear.

"Are you okay, Tammy?" asked a voice at the other end. Finally, at long last, Paul's sister.

"I fine. You heer now?"

"No. You're in the wrong place."

"Rong place?"

"Yes, we don't know exactly how it happened, but you're at Baltimore International Airport and you should be here at St. Louis International. Somehow, we're not sure exactly how, but you landed in Maryland, Tammy. You're a long ways from St. Louis."

"Wha!" Tammy's gaze darted between the airport employees who nodded their agreement.

"But we'll get you back. Don't worry, the airport staff will take care of you. They said they'll fix everything."

Paul's sister chattered on, something about how frantically they had all looked for her . . . police notified . . . security guards searching St. Louis International . . . everyone worried . . .

But quick on the heels of her relief, Tammy's thoughts raced. *You mean America has* another *airport?* She mentally ticked them off: *Honolulu, San Francisco, St. Louis—and now Baltimore.* Four airports! What a large country she had come to.

The phone call ended after more reassurances, and the lady behind the ticket counter explained they had already arranged for her to catch the next TWA flight to St. Louis at 8:00 p.m. that same night.

"You come back to this counter, okay? Come right here and we'll see to everything." The clerk patted Tammy's hand.

Tammy nodded, suddenly drained, faint. Faint and hungry.

Hungry? She was starved!

She reached into her wallet, grabbed a few dollar bills and treated herself to her first meal in America: a hot dog and coffee.

CHAPTER 16

Off-Base Apartment, 1973–74
Fort Meade, Maryland

Food for Thought

A confusing but warm flurry of sisters, welcomes and wedding plans greeted Tammy in St. Louis.

"There's not a thing for you to do." Paul's mother put her arm around Tammy's shoulder. "We've taken care of it all. The church, the preacher, the party. It's all done, so you don't have to worry."

Worry? Why should she worry? She thought about the wedding celebrations she had attended as a girl, always the responsibility of the groom's family. Shrugging, Tammy eyed Virginia—a stocky Missouri housewife who had birthed twelve children and whose gray hair crowned a face sweet and gentle—and liked her immediately, certain she would come to love her American mother-in-law.

"Dickie," Virginia said, "you'll need to take Tammy to get your blood tests taken care of."

Blood? They wanted her blood? Whatever for? Tammy flinched. And . . . *Dickie?*

"Who Dic-ee?" Tammy asked.

"Me," said Paul.

She whipped her head around to look at him. "Wha? Wha are you nam?"

"Well, my full name is Paul Richard Fadler. But my family calls me Dick. Or Dickie."

Tammy stiffened. He had another name and hadn't bothered to tell her?

Virginia, oblivious to Tammy's reaction, kept up a steady stream of conversation. ". . . and then you'll take her to the courthouse to get a license."

Wait a minute. Weren't courthouses for criminals? Tammy shook her head ruefully. She wasn't in Saigon anymore, but she would learn. She would learn.

At the courthouse, Paul . . . Dickie . . . *Dick* told Tammy they needed to wait for his parents to arrive.

"You paren? Why for we nee paren?" she asked, worried because her own couldn't be in attendance.

"To sign papers."

"Pay-per? Why for?"

"For permission," he snapped. "Legally, I'm not old enough so I need their permission."

"I tot sam age. You say sam."

"Yeh, well, not exactly." Dick looked down, squinting at the toes of his shoes. "I'm, uh, a year younger than you."

Younger! Tammy fumed. She'd never wanted to marry someone younger than her. Always, the friends she had been drawn to were older than she was. As a matter of fact, Khai was several years older, wise and worldly. As the eldest child of a large family, she'd matured early. She'd had her fill of looking after those younger than herself. And, now, a young husband!

Who was this man, anyway? Paul or Dick? Same age or younger? A man who would look after her or another child she needed to provide for? She tried to temper her thoughts and rein in her anger.

The next two weeks whirred by in a haze.

Tammy knew the pink silk gown she had made before leaving Saigon flattered her eighty-nine pound silhouette. Would Dick think so, too? Although a French influence was evident in the heart-shaped neckline, she fancied the straight cut and long sleeves gave it an American look. She hoped he noticed.

She stood with pride before Dick, his family and a scattering of their friends for the short ceremony at the Baptist church. It happened so fast, though, she hardly remembered it.

Tammy felt comfortable with Dick's large family and Sunday dinner at the farm where everyone gathered each weekend after the wedding—all the brothers and sisters and in-laws, the nieces and nephews living in the area—with Virginia cooking for the entire battalion, not unlike Sundays in Khan Hoi with her own family.

Well, maybe not *exactly* the same as home. Tammy watched in bewilderment when the men crowded the table, Dick's dad Floyd at the head, leaving no seats for the women and children. She questioned her mother-in-law.

"The table won't hold us all, so we do two dinner seatings," Virginia pointed out reasonably.

"But, why not you fee chil-ren fir, Mom?"

"Cuz," Floyd interrupted in a no-nonsense tone, "the men eat first." He picked between his back teeth with the nail of his smallest finger, eyed the sliver of beef he dislodged and flicked it onto his plate. "That's the way things are done here." He rolled his tongue around his gums and smacked his lips. "Not to worry, kiddo, we saved enough for you." He winked at a son-in-law across the table and chortled.

Tammy thought of home, where no adult would ever consider eating before sating the hungry bellies of the youngest in the family. Her gaze swung past his brothers to Dick chewing a bite of roast. She waited for him to swallow, to say something to Floyd. He didn't even look up.

Tammy scowled at her father-in-law. "Keep you foo. I no hon-gree."

She stalked out the door.

✦ ✦ ✦

After a belated wedding trip to meet more family in Arizona, Dick took Tammy back with him to Fort Meade where his friends, Ken and Joyce, offered to rent them a bedroom in their apartment until married housing opened on base, an arrangement that benefited both young couples who were struggling to make ends meet.

One day, concern pinched Joyce's brow as she eyed Tammy's thin clothing. "We've got to find you something warmer. And soon." She turned to burrow in the back of her closet. "Meanwhile, I know I have an extra . . . Here. I'd like to give you this."

She held the knee-length coat while Tammy slid her arms into the sleeves and fumbled at the buttons.

"Hurry up, Tammy! You won't want to miss this!" their husbands yelled from the front door.

Eager to embrace a new adventure, Tammy stepped into the yard. Pivoting on her heels, she made a complete circle to view this wonder. Winter had found a coat of her own.

Snow!

Snow falling as soft and silent as the down of a peahen. It floated around her in a show that seemed oddly hushed, private, meant only for her eyes, for her senses.

White fluff drifted around her, covering everything—trees and cars, buildings and bushes, sidewalks and stoops. She cupped her hand to catch the flakes, flakes so light, so weightless, she couldn't feel them until they melted in the warmth of her palm, leaving tiny puddles of cold. She caught more and, before they could melt again, dabbed the point of her tongue against them for a taste, fancying they were as sweet as the shaved-ice desserts sold in the markets of Saigon.

She dipped up handfuls to toss, shook the branches of low trees and tall bushes, remembering that she had seen snow somewhere before. Of course, in the movie *Holiday Inn* at Long Binh! Why hadn't anyone told her how amazing it felt, how pristine it made the world, how cold and clean and . . .

Splat!

"Whhhaaa?" Tammy shook her head, brushing the snow from her hair, and whipped around to see Dick's laughing face.

He bent for a second scoop, mounding it between his hands and warned, "Arm yourself, woman. Here comes another one!"

Tammy ducked, just in time.

Shrieking neighborhood kids swarmed from the surrounding apartment buildings, challenging each other to snowball fights, teaming up to build snow forts and plopping in the powder to flap their arms.

"Wha dey do?" she asked Dick.

"Snow angels." He pointed. "Watch what happens when they stand up."

Not content to be a spectator, Tammy tugged the brown fur collar tighter against her neck, pulling it up to warm her ears, and was soon rolling in the snow with the giggling kids.

✦ ✦ . ✦

Word by word, day by day, week by week, Tammy was absorbing American culture as quickly as a dried mushroom in water. She found herself noticing its oddities, wading through its nuances, determining its differences. From the moment she had arrived, she opened herself to accept and adopt this new life.

Ever worried about income, Tammy decided it was time to look for work.

I can always cook, she thought.

She landed a job at a nearby diner and received her first paycheck: $6.18. After handing Dick six dollars so he could get gas for his car, she pocketed the loose change and headed to the PX. Joyce needed sugar and Tammy felt she should buy it for her.

As she wandered through the merchandise, Tammy eyed a prominent display of sweets. *Chocolate.* Her stomach growled; her mouth watered. How long had it been since she'd had the luxury of a chocolate bar? Without a thought, she grabbed one from the top of the rack, located a packet of sugar for Joyce and made her way to the checkout counter.

"How much thih?" She showed the clerk her items.

"Fifteen cents for the sugar. Ten cents for the candy bar."

With a philosophical shrug, Tammy reached for the coins in her purse. She left the PX with only the packet of sugar. Sacrifice was nothing new to her.

Several months later, Joyce approached Tammy after supper while the two washed dishes.

"Today at work, I heard about an opening. I would love to recommend you, if you'd like me to." The soft-spoken woman looked up. "Would you be interested?"

Tammy tried to keep her face composed, but . . . a job at the sewing factory?

Ugh. No thank you.

"It's piecework, you know."

Piecework? Do I know piecework?

She shuddered at the memory of her younger self snipping off buttons and picking out zippers and ripping apart seams of the Red Cross donations before separating and sorting and piling them—piece by piece by dreary piece—under Aunt Three's critical eye.

I despised sewing then, I despise it now.

She opened her mouth to reject the offer.

"You can make pretty good money, you know," Joyce added.

Tammy's head whipped around. "Goo mon-nee?" At Joyce's nod, she put down her dish towel. "Tell me moh!"

Under contract with the government, C.R. Daniels provided the military with belts, canteen covers, munition casings and knapsacks made out of camouflage and canvas. The factory was nearby. The work was steady.

And the pay? The pay?

"The better you sew, the faster you work . . ."

Tammy shook the wrinkles out of her sewing skills, applied for the job and ably learned the intricacies of the industrial machine assigned to her.

Piecework at C.R. Daniels, she learned, meant getting paid for each piece she produced during the day. After the minimum was met, she received extra money for every item she sewed. The more she sewed, the more she earned.

More earnings?

Tammy needed no other motivation to master the trade. The clarion call of Ma's mantra spanned the ocean to narrow her choices: *You do, or you don't eat.*

Even after such a short time away from them, Tammy found her thoughts turning more and more often to her family. The loved ones she had left behind. Parents, sisters, brothers who—though they might "do"—didn't always have much to eat. She worried that, without income from her, things had gotten even worse. Well, *she* could do.

Feeling guilty about her own high standard of living, she tucked small bills into each letter home, five dollars today, ten dollars another time. Last week, twenty. No one would go hungry; Ma knew how to stretch money.

Tammy *had*, so she gave.

After all, Saigon might be called the Pearl of the East; but in her eyes, America was the Diamond of the World, the Land of Milk and Honey *and* the Land of Opportunity. America was more than she had ever imagined.

It teemed with prospects. Possibilities. Potential.

America, she knew, was a place where anyone, even a young, uneducated Vietnamese woman, might make something of herself.

What would it take, she wondered, *to bring them all here?* To have her entire family with her? In America? The thought teased her waking hours and wove colorful visions through her sleep.

When she heard about an opening at another factory, Tammy was the first to apply for a job making clothing. The sewing was more interesting, the work cleaner and the pay higher. She even had time in the evenings to take advantage of the language tutoring offered at Fort Meade.

Seeing a pressing need for English assistance to accommodate Vietnamese brides, a couple of officers' wives had organized regular classes. Tammy favored the Major's wife with her soft Mississippi drawl, who worked with her so patiently, helping with that most difficult of difficult words to pronounce: Thread. A stringy word to chew.

The tutor lengthened it, slowing to draw out each letter sound.

Th-r-e-ad.

Th . . . r . . . eh-ad.

Thhh . . . rrr . . . ehh . . . add.

"Thread. Ya see? It's not so hard. Now, y'all try it."

The soft *th* sound combined with a rolled *r* was foreign to Tammy's tongue. But the dear woman willingly repeated the entire process, praising Tammy as she got closer and closer to saying it right.

Tonight, she vowed, *tonight I'll say it correctly.*

"Where ya goin'?" Dick asked from the couch where he sprawled in front of the television set.

She paused at the front door. "To ler goo Een-lish."

"Again?" He gritted his teeth. "Forget the classes. Ya talk fine."

Khai would never say something like that. He would support me. Tammy swallowed against the thought. Khai was part of another life, the life she'd left behind when she climbed on the plane for America. She had chosen Dick.

Her hand tightened on her purse, but her husband wasn't finished. "You work long hours at the factory, then you're out the door for the whole night. Why can't you just stay home like the other women in my family?"

Her jaw clenched.

Things were different in this country. She understood that. Even so, Tammy had hoped for, well, for more than she was getting from Dick. A little softness, certainly. Some interest, maybe. And simple encouragement would be nice. She sighed. Perhaps it was time to set aside her girlish notions of romance; those foolish ideas belonged to her past. She needed to face this new life head on.

She turned the doorknob. "I wone be lay. Okay?"

Dick didn't bother to answer.

She thought about the words she wanted to say to her husband, then, taking a deep breath, chose, instead, to repeat the ones she had just uttered. Tammy sounded them out, testing her lessons and new prowess.

"I won'T be laTe," she enunciated.

She stepped out the door, shutting it behind her with enough firmness to punctuate the sentence.

CHAPTER 17

PX, April 30, 1975
Fort Meade, Maryland

Left Behind

Tammy and Dick wandered the busy PX, poking through merchandise, browsing through clothes, picking up an item here and there on their shopping list. Dick hummed along a phrase or two while "Love Will Keep Us Together" spilled from the intercom, stopping only to examine a new Kodak Tele-Instamatic.

"Twenty-eight bucks!" He whistled under his breath before putting it back on the shelf to only reach for another model. "Is there anything else ya need for your trip, Tammy?"

She thought a minute before shaking her head; she would travel nearly as lightly back to Vietnam as she'd arrived here eighteen months ago. Besides, she wouldn't leave until early June, so there was plenty of time yet. But the mere thought of visiting family and friends made her heart race, her step lighten.

Letters from home assured her that, even without an American presence, the SVNA was in control, skirmishes less frequent. Like an unruly child who was finally tamed, the war seemed to have calmed. It would be, they all agreed, a good time for her to come. Tammy worked and scrimped for months to save enough money for a plane ticket back, making plans to see everyone, Ba and Ma and Vui, Hoa and Susie and . . .

". . . to put down their weapons . . ." crackled the loudspeaker from somewhere inside the PX.

Dick's head whipped around. "Did you hear that?"

"Heer wha . . ."

Dick silenced her with a wave of his palm.

"It's over . . . called for surrender. Minh, acting president of South Vietnam for only the last three days declared the . . ."

The underlying drone in the commissary quieted. The Captain and Tennille were silenced. Cashiers paused their registers. Conversations stopped mid-sentence. An expectant hush settled over the entire PX. Tammy clutched her heart and held her breath, straining to listen, fearful she might miss a word.

"The North Vietnamese Army took over Saigon with little resistance."

Tammy gasped and groped blindly for Dick's hand.

"President Minh announced the surrender of the city."

"Nooooooo," she groaned.

Her family! What about Ba and Ma and the others?

An immense weight crushed her chest and wrung the last of the air from her lungs. She flailed for a breath, just one, to ease the tightness that was suffocating her.

A man behind her moaned. "But my wife! My son! I'm still trying to get them here!"

His agony underscored her own deep pain. Tammy sucked in more air and whirled to face him. "My fam-ee too. My fam-ee too."

Reaching out, his eyes awash with tears, the black soldier drew her into the crush of his arms. "I'm so sorry. So, so sorry." He cried.

She clung to him, sobbing.

Tammy felt Dick step forward to embrace them both: his Vietnamese wife who had left everyone behind in a country now held by the Communists; this heartbroken soldier whose own Vietnamese wife and child were still there, caught behind enemy lines, hemmed in by a power larger than them all.

We've all lost, she thought. *We've all lost.*

That evening, Tammy and Dick clustered around the television with Ken and Joyce, not really talking, still trying to absorb everything.

Scenes flashed across the screen:

A PAVN tank crashing through the gates of the Presidential Palace . . . The rooftop evacuation of the U.S. Embassy . . . A human chain of South Vietnamese nationals scrambling to board an Air America helicopter . . . A Marine crewman carrying a Vietnamese toddler to safety –

Hoa! Tammy realized she had nearly forgotten about her cousin. *What will happen to her now?* She recalled their meeting, after John and Dick were sent back to the States.

Sitting over coffee at their favorite Saigon café, Hoa had toyed with her drink.

"I'm pregnant," she finally blurted.

Tammy didn't flinch. Many of the girls who worked on military bases, where tips were steep and friendships came with a price, found themselves in the same predicament. "What are you going to do?"

Hoa shifted her shoulders in resignation. "I'll do whatever I need to."

"You'll keep the baby, then?"

Hoa nodded. "I'll keep it."

Silence wrapped around the two friends until Tammy voiced the question that needed to be asked. "What about John?"

Hoa hunched over the table. Swirled her cold coffee. "He'll come for me. For us." She stared into the depths of her cup and took a deep breath. Exhaled. "He'll come. John will come and take me and the baby to America."

But John hadn't returned, not yet. And now he couldn't.

Tammy thought about the mournful soldier in the PX. She thought about John and Hoa. She thought about Ma and Ba. *So many families torn apart.*

She forced herself to refocus on the television screen, where the South Vietnamese flag was yanked down, a new flag raised.

A sadness, deeper than anything she could imagine, infiltrated Tammy's soul at the sudden lack of identity she felt. Her home and her heritage had vanished when that flag came down. She felt as though she had been violated, stripped and ravaged. She knew she had been robbed of something . . . precious. She was now, officially, a woman without a country.

I guess I'm still Vietnamese, after all, she thought.

The two couples continued to stare at the set, trying to absorb the full impact of Saigon's chaotic fall.

More scenes flickered by: refugees fleeing the advance of Communist forces . . . a jeering crowd with the strangely serene head of a demolished statue . . . mobs scaling the fourteen-foot wall of the U.S. Embassy in Saigon . . . soldiers shedding shirts and pants, baring themselves to tee shirts and boxers, tossing away their identifying uniforms as they fled . . .

Bile rose in Tammy's throat at the bitter sight of a proud military so diminished.

She knew others would not shed their uniforms so easily. Why, Khai would face the enemy, face certain execution rather than—

Khai!

Tammy's heart caught, held, a captive to his memory.

Khai!

Where was he in all this mayhem?

Dead?

No! Not dead, surely not dead.

Hadn't the telecasters reported that President Minh offered a ceremonious transfer of power in order to avoid bloodshed?

No, not dead. Never dead.

If Khai were dead, she would know, wouldn't she? Somewhere, deep inside her being, she would most certainly know.

"I'll find you. No matter what," he had vowed.

Tammy glanced at Dick from the corner of her eye and flushed. She focused again on the newscast and its closing shot. A black-and-white photograph, silent and still, one identical to countless others taken repeatedly during the war. But that didn't lessen its wrenching impact.

It depicted a sort of, well—a memorial. An altar.

Grim rows of M-16 rifles stood at rigid attention in a clearing, bayonet ends piercing the ground like scarecrows in a field. A helmet topped each rifle and, placed with precision at the foot of every one . . . an empty pair of combat boots.

The television camera zoomed in for a closeup: one helmeted rifle, one pair of empty boots.

The camera paused.

Lingered.

And faded to black.

CHAPTER 18

On the Streets, 1975
Fort Meade, Maryland

Bingo!

A crisp breeze fanned Tammy's cheeks when they stepped outside. She lagged behind Dick to inhale the tang of fall, knowing that, even in the dark, trees danced to a chorus of color. She loved the way the vibrant leaves—eggplant purple, brilliant pumpkin and rambutan red—shimmied to the ground, covering it with a thick, crackling mat. Autumn was a season she had neither recognized nor celebrated in Vietnam, and Tammy thought she would never tire of the season's showy promenade.

"How 'bout you drive us home for a change?" Dick tossed her the keys and slid into the passenger seat of his souped-up Camaro.

"But, it geh-teen dar ouw."

"Ya need to learn sometime and now's as good a time as any. Even in the dark."

He was right. She did need to practice driving. Even so, they'd just finished a late evening of bingo, she had never driven when it was this black outside and, besides, her learner's permit was still garden-fresh. Dick closed his door. Resigned, she climbed into the driver's seat.

"Remember what I told ya. One foot on the gas, the other on the clutch, *then* turn the key."

She remembered. Tammy started the car without a hitch and nudged its nose into the street. With Dick's prompts, she managed a smoother drive than some in the recent past. So smooth, in fact, she was finding a degree of comfort behind the wheel and more than a little pride in her achievement.

When he said, "Shift," she shifted.

When he said, "Stop sign coming up," she braked.

And she kept her foot on the clutch to keep the car idling until he said, "Put it into first." Which she did.

Consequently, the drive home through leaf-crusted streets was uneventful. Until, that is, she slowed to a crawl and squinted through the shadows to find the right-hand turn into the tight parking lot of the one-room efficiency apartment they had recently acquired.

"Down shift, Tammy," Dick reminded her, too late.

The Camaro stalled.

Tammy restarted it, but when she tried to inch forward into the narrow turn, the car stuttered, stopped again.

"Ya need to give it more gas," said Dick.

She dried her clammy palms against her pant legs and gave it more gas, but the car lurched when she let out the clutch, and the engine died. Flustered, she immediately tried again;

but this time, the Camaro tossed its head with a defiant jerk and refused to even kick in.

"One foot on the gas pedal, the other on the clutch, *then* turn the key. Remember?" Dick's voice held more than a hint of impatience.

Tammy leaned her forehead against the upper edge of the steering wheel. "Why dohn you par it?" Her voice was muffled, pleading.

"No, *you* need to learn how to park. Ya have to finish this, Tammy."

She started the car once more and eased her left foot from the clutch.

"Now, Tammy, gas!" Dick yelled. "Give it some gas!"

Tammy gave it some gas. When she stomped on the pedal, the Camaro jumped over the curb, into the lot—making a nose dive straight into the side of their neighbor's car—and shoved that car into the vehicle parked on the other side of it. And shoved *that* vehicle mighty close to a third.

The Camaro landed with a shudder and bucked to a heavy stop. Tammy and Dick sat in stunned silence. Tammy had, indeed, parked the car.

At long last, Dick reached over to turn off the key.

"Are ya okay?"

She nodded.

"Ya sure?" He sighed. "Well, let me have a look."

She nodded once more, unwilling to trust her voice. As soon as Dick got out to assess the damage, she burst into tears.

Another bill! she thought. *How will I ever pay for repairs?*

Dick loved his muscle car with its suspended rear axle and external modifications. He admired the sleekness built into his fully loaded, 1967 Camaro. It seemed designed for racing and the Corvette engine he'd installed made it even faster. So race it he did. All over Fort Meade. She ought to know.

How many speeding tickets has he gotten? Too many to count. The last handful ate her entire paycheck—all $140 of it—money better saved than spent, especially for such irresponsible behavior.

Money wasted on speeding tickets, she sputtered, righteous indignation overshadowing any hint of guilt she might have felt for crashing the car her husband worshipped. *So much money wasted, when I'm working my hardest for those in dire need of food and shelter. How dare his car eat the money that could feed my family!*

Suddenly, she realized Dick was calling to her. Standing next to him was the MP. Tammy brushed the moisture from her cheeks, smoothed her long hair and composed herself before opening the door and stepping from the car to join them. Resentful leaves scattered at her feet.

She wasn't worried, not really. Every officer of the Military Police on base knew this royal-blue bullet. In fact, Dick swore they all kept track of him for the explicit joy of issuing yet another ticket.

They'll probably be pleased to see his Camaro out of business at last, she thought with a tinge of satisfaction.

"You the one who did this?" The MP pointed with the end of his pen, sweeping across the furrowed fenders, damaged doors and battered front ends.

Her eyes widened at the extent of damage. She lowered her head and nodded, meek. Subdued.

The MP scribbled in his notebook. "You have a license?"

She dug her driving permit from her purse and handed it to him.

“You been drinking tonight?” He avoided making eye contact.

She shook her head with adamant denial. “No!”

“No? You sure?”

“I shure.”

Dick, she noticed with concern, had turned his back to them and stood there, his shoulders shaking.

“Okay. Then, I have just one final question for you, Ma’am.” The MP looked at the Camaro, cleared his throat, and elbowed Dick. Her husband turned around and both men snickered out loud.

“Just how the hell,” the MP snorted and lost himself in a bellowing laugh, “did you ever manage to park this thing?”

And that’s when she looked, really looked, at Dick’s car.

She had managed to park it in the small lot, all right. She’d parked the loaded Camaro with efficiency. She’d parked it snugly. Horizontally. Across two vertical spaces. Spaces she’d opened wide by merely . . . giving it some gas.

▲ First job with the U.S. military, Huỳnh Thị Thuận, age fifteen—*and a half*

▲ Thuận, a salad-maker, in 1966

▲ Thuận as kitchen helper at the Main Officer Club, Long Bình, 1968

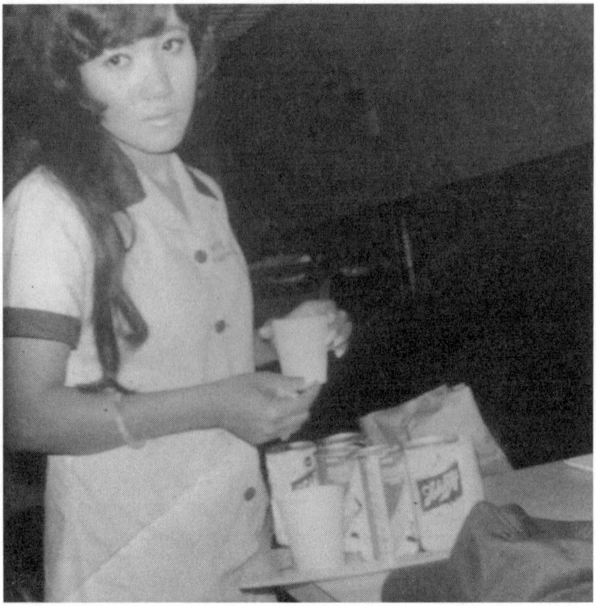

◀ Long Bình Post, 1970, Thuận waitressing

▲ Last family photo with her siblings before flying to America, 1973. From left: Sister Two: Thuận; Sister Three: Vui; Brother Four: Hiệp; Sister Five: Xuân; Brother Six: Tâm; Brother Seven: Nghĩa; Brother Eight: Thành; Sister Nine: Hương; Brother Ten: Công; Brother Eleven: Đức; Brother Twelve: Hạnh

▲The Fadler family at the Fadler farmhouse, Festus, Missouri

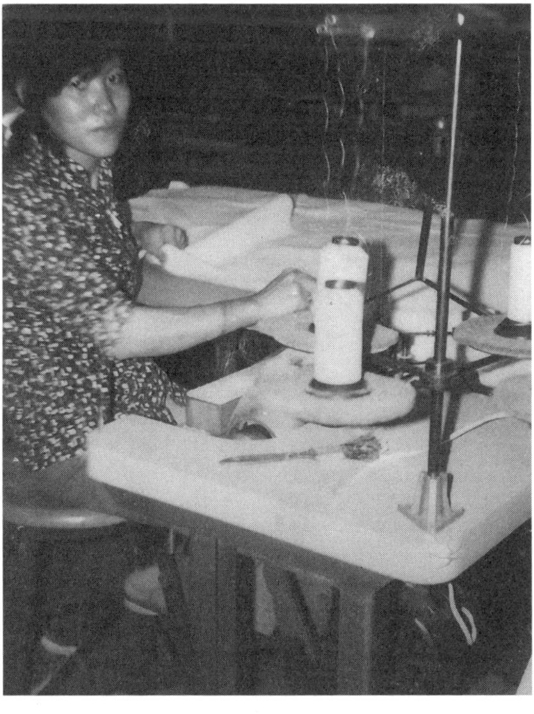

◀Tammy Fadler sewing for C.R. Daniels

Mall Street Journal   Mall Street Journal

Tammy Fadler...#1 Citizen

Tammy Fadler was pleasently surprised last week when her fellow employees gave a party in her honor to celebrate her new citizenship....
Tammy came to the United States from Viet Nam five years ago. She met and married Paul Fadler while he was on tour in her native country.

Like any other true American she is learning to like hot dogs, apple pie and MCDonald hamburgers....
"I can vote now, Tammy said, "but never for my boss Joe Blow, he is too good a boss and that would mean I would loss him to an election."
Tammy is employed at Goldes in the Twin CIty Mall as a seamstress in the alteration department.

The Fadlers live in Festus with their two year old daughter...

Golde Employees and manager Joe Blow helped surprise Tammy to honor her naturalization

▲ Citizenship celebration with Joe Blow and friends at Golde's Department Store, Festus, Missouri

▲ Việt Nam in 1981, Ba and Má at Sister Five's wedding

▲ Ginny and Richie in front of the $18,000 house, Easter of 1982

▲ Tammy and her beloved Saigon Restaurant

▲ Fellow agents with Century 21 Showcase host Tammy's college graduation party

◀ Tammy featured in her despised Century 21 gold jacket

▼ Dorothy Rodriguez, Rick Ramsey and Tammy, RE/MAX team

▲Ginny and Richie, marketing photo at Tammy's RE/MAX office

▲Typical day, Tammy at Signature Properties

▼Joyous reunion at Lambert International Airport after Tammy sponsors Huỳnh family members to the U.S.

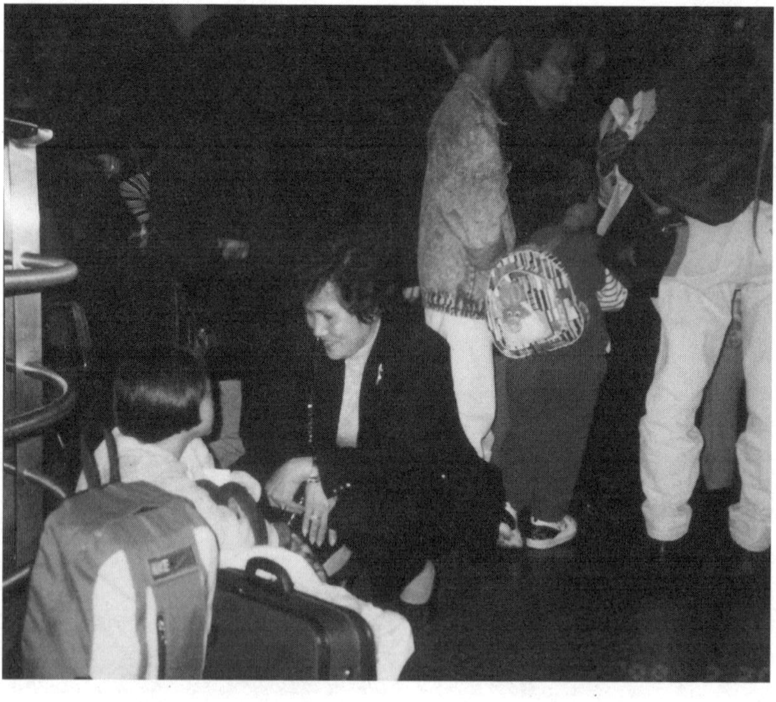

Vietnamese dong

▲ Tân Sơn Nhứt Airport, 2001, Brother Seven holding sign welcoming Tammy—Sister Two

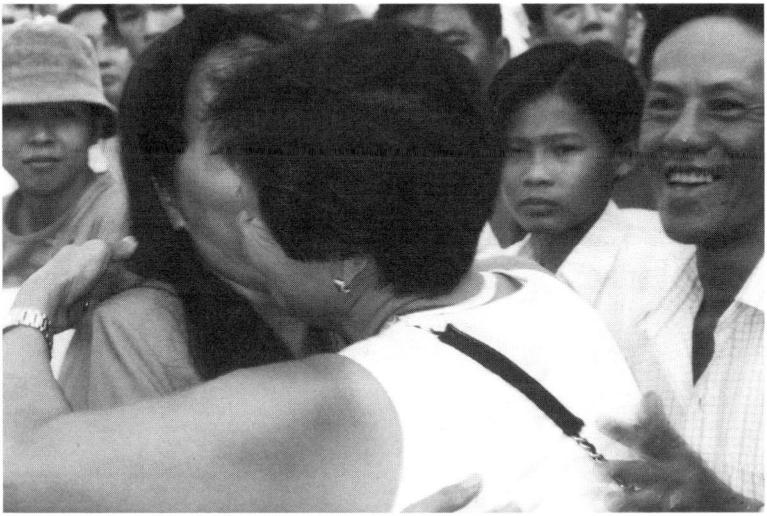

▲ Tammy meeting Brother Seven's wife for the first time and embracing Brother Seven

▲ Leaving Tân Sơn Nhứt Airport—Tuesday Sister Glenda Williamson, Sister-in-law Number Seven, Tammy, Uncle Five and Brother Seven

▲ After her twenty-eight-year absence, Tammy spends time with Brother Seven

▼ Khánh Hội street scenes, Tammy's first return trip to Việt Nam, 2001

▲Brother Seven, Nghĩa, at work on the streets of Sài Gòn

▲Tammy (center) at the 12′X12′ home of Aunt Four and Uncle Six, her father's siblings

▲Entrance to the fish market in Khánh Hội where Tammy sold fish as a child

▲Brunching at the Renaissance with Nick and Gail French and Glenda Williamson, Tammy shares childhood memories

CHAPTER 19

Fadler Farmhouse, 1976
Festus, Missouri

Bare Necessities

Tammy tossed her books on the kitchen table. Algebra, English and history texts thudded against the Formica top.

Did she really say that? Did she say I shouldn't have come to America? Tammy fumed. *What was that woman thinking? And, why would she say that about me?*

After Dick's discharge from the Army last September when they had moved from Fort Meade to Missouri to live with his parents, and she thought every one of the five thousand residents in Festus welcomed her. Isolated from bustling St. Louis by an hour-long drive, the rural community felt warm and intimate. She certainly hadn't expected a particular neighbor's cold-shoulder treatment and unkind remarks.

Oh, she knew she was different. She didn't look like her neighbors, she didn't dress like them and she didn't speak like them. Even so, to hint that she wasn't welcome, that she had married Dick only to get out of Vietnam, that she had no business being here—merely because she wasn't exactly like them?

"Con sâu có thể làm hư nồi canh," she whispered to the empty walls of the farmhouse kitchen. "One worm can ruin the entire pot of soup."

On the contrary, she was quick to admit that she'd been on the receiving end of goodness and kindness from so many. Frightened about her impending motherhood and worried about being fully responsible for the precious baby growing inside her, Tammy had felt so alone at Fort Meade with no mother to answer questions, no sisters to offer assistance. She knew she needed to surround herself with women, loving and able. So, it had been an easy decision to move to Festus, where she would have help from Dick's eager mom and willing older sisters, all of them excited about the baby they would be welcoming to their large, extended family.

In addition, as the first Vietnamese war bride to appear in this rural Missouri town, Tammy had been embraced without reserve when she applied at a small, local dry cleaner for work.

"You nee sew-een? I do sew-een. Bery, bery goo sew-een."

Although she was drawing some unemployment after their move from Maryland, until Dick could find a job, there would be no other income for their growing family. Her pregnancy now visibly evident, Tammy knew no one in Festus would hire her and offer the coveted benefit of medical insurance. She chose to look for something she could do at home with the old sewing machine Dick's mom loaned for her use.

Tammy rolled up her shirt sleeves and, once again utilizing the despised sewing skills taught her by Aunt Three, offered to do alterations for a local dry cleaner. Pleased with her work and responsiveness to their needs, the cleaner soon gave Tammy all their business and, as her reputation spread, she began accepting work from the other dry cleaner business in Festus, as well.

Feeling more secure with money coming into the household, Tammy valiantly tried to adjust to country living: Sparrows strung across telephone wires framing the pastoral woods and fields where Mom and Floyd, caretakers of the farm, had raised cattle, chickens and a herd of children. Their well-tended garden stretched across the yard, burgeoning with pungent onions, blazing squashes and plump tomatoes. But Tammy was a city girl at heart. Besides, she decided, she didn't want to spend the rest of her life doing the manual labor that defined both her family and Dick's. She was determined to elevate herself in this, the golden Land of Opportunity.

An old Vietnamese proverb came to mind: *If you want to travel fast, use the old roads.*

That's it! she thought. *Education was always the only way out of poverty in Vietnam. Education will most certainly be my ticket to success here in America.*

She decided to get the schooling she'd yearned for since she was a young child. She would seek knowledge. She would improve her lot in life. She would, *she would* get a high-school diploma!

Tammy nodded decisively. Turning to the new family she had embraced, she asked for their support.

"I'd love to baby sit for you," encouraged her sister-in-law, Judy.

"I'll help, too, with the baby after it's born," offered her sweet mother-in-law. "Then you'll have time for homework." They had adopted each other, it seemed; Tammy because she needed a mother and Mom because she had a big heart with room to spare.

"There, now. It's settled." Mom folded her thick arms across her waist.

Tammy eyed Dick, still jobless, where he sprawled in the living room of his parents' farmhouse.

"You're always looking for something more," he grouched from his dad's worn armchair. "Nothing is ever enough for ya, is it?" He turned his attention back to the television show she'd interrupted.

Undaunted, Tammy decided to obtain a coveted GED. With only a little investigation on her part, she found out how to enroll in the evening classes offered through Festus High School.

"Wha this cos?" she asked at registration.

"Cost? Why nothing," she was told. "It's free."

Free education, available to everyone just for the asking, Tammy marveled, startled that the classes weren't packed, surprised that more people weren't taking advantage of the menu of courses. Apparently, the only thing they needed to do was show up and claim a desk.

"An . . . ih *free*," she muttered, shaking her head in disbelief. A person didn't even need to have money to attend.

The burnished bricks of Festus High School glowed in the early evening light. She paused at the sidewalk until she felt the low-slung building beckon, arms outstretched to pull her inside where books stood in stacks and knowledge flowed as generously as the warm maple syrup Mom poured on her morning pancakes.

Like Tammy, the other students were adults who, for one reason or another, had never completed their education.

Unlike her, they were American and they all spoke English, fluent English.

Tammy realized right away that she was in trouble. She couldn't understand the assignments or follow the discussions as well as she needed to complete her homework. Soft-spoken Mrs. Genevieve Holligan, who headed the continuing-education program, saw Tammy's struggles and understood her intense desire to learn.

"Come with me," the tall woman urged. "Let's see what we can do to make this easier for you."

Mrs. Holligan escorted her down the hallway to the library.

"There are some books I think will help with your language skills. Let me see if I can find them for you." She turned away to search a shelf. "I believe this would be a good one. And maybe this one . . ."

Tammy strolled around the large room, running her index finger down the spines of book after book after book. *Shelves of books!* She shook her head in awe. *So many books. So much to learn.* Her heart soared.

"Tammy." Mrs. Holligan motioned her over. "I'd like you to meet two of our teachers, Phyllis Forrest and Willa McCullough. I've recruited them to tutor you in English. Go to Willa with any difficulties you might have in her class. You'll meet with Phyllis outside of the classroom. This way, you'll be able to keep up with the other students."

Humbled that so many people were willing to offer their time and assistance to a foreign woman from an alien land, Tammy felt her eyes mist.

She sucked in her breath at a sudden vivid memory of Vietnam. Of a time, not so long ago, that she'd had an opportunity to offer assistance to "foreigners," too.

She had first read about them through the Sài Gòn newspaper, a group of people she'd never heard about before—people she'd never known existed—who lived in the jungled mountains of her own country.

Startlingly primitive, Montagnard tribes from the Central Highlands of Việt Nam had allied themselves with U.S. forces against the invading Việt Cộng. With a well-earned reputation for bravery and combat skill, the "Yards" fought beside American Special Forces in cross-border operations.

And the Communists made certain they paid a steep price for their allegiance to the South.

This upland minority, skilled artisans, escaped their bombed and ravaged villages, deserting their burning houses-on-stilts, their livelihoods and their handicrafts. Along with their children, their frail elderly and their elephants, they were herded to refugee camps.

Compassion overwhelmed Tammy as she pondered these indigenous people. When she discovered there was a refugee camp north of Long Bình in dire need of supplies, she mounted a campaign to raise money for the bare necessities that were lacking: rice and sugar, whatever other food she might be able to transport. What was it Ông Thầy had taught them as school children? *Giving a crumb to the hungry is of more worth than giving lunch to the satisfied.* To her delight, she discovered that most people understood and practiced that same principle. Nearly everyone she approached on base was willing to contribute to the cause.

Her co-workers at the NCO Club donated their hard-earned tips; GIs dug deep into their pockets; her bosses added to the growing fund.

She found others willing to help, as well. Someone provided boxes. Someone donated a civilian truck. Someone else found a driver. Others volunteered to load and unload. And they all headed north on National Highway 1.

Tammy stepped from the truck and surveyed the camp. Montagnards were everywhere, parents without children and children without parents. When men and boys crowded around the truck, her eyes widened in fascination at her first glimpse of these primitive people. They looked—different. Different from everyone she knew in Sài Gòn. Their skin was dark. Their hair was bound tightly. Their clothing was cut in a style unfamiliar to a city girl like her. The women wore long, wrapped skirts topped with . . .

Tammy blinked. Gasped. Blinked again.

There are no tops.

There. Are. No. Tops.

She pivoted on her heels, casting a piercing stare around the busy camp of Montagnards.

Breasts swung loose and flat against the emaciated ribs of a tiny elderly woman. A contented baby suckled at the full breasts of his weary mother. A teenager stirred a pot of rice, one ripe orb pressed against her slender arm. Young girls romped in an open field, their budding chests bare in the blushing morning light.

No tops, she confirmed.

Embarrassed that someone might notice her staring, Tammy turned back to the truck to oversee the unloading. No one else, she determined, acted like anything was out of the ordinary. Still amazed, she couldn't seem to control her gaze as it occasionally darted around the refugee camp.

Apparently, she decided, there was one *bare* necessity she had neglected to bring: clothing. She would see to it that the next truckload came with tops.

Plenty of tops.

Tammy grinned at the memory—and her own naïveté. She placed the palm of her hand against the algebra text on the kitchen table, recalling the delicious, book-lined library of Festus High School and the warm eyes of the three women so willing to meet her needs. To teach her, tutor her and mentor her.

They had been willing—in spite of her differences.

They had been willing—in spite of her foreignness.

Once, Tammy had provided food for people in need. Now she was the recipient of good deeds. And she was, quite simply, grateful for these women teachers and tutors who were so willing to feed the hunger that gnawed within her.

Chapter 20

Fadler Farmhouse, Summer 1979
Festus, Missouri

House Bound

Mom and Floyd's weathered white farmhouse squatted at the end of the gravel road, anchoring the property with its two-story frame, arthritic with age. Nearby sprawled an equally gnarled garage next to a rusting gasoline tank and, behind, a low-slung garden where tendrils of sweet peas tickled thick cucumbers, and stalks of tall corn marched in rows, their friendly tasseled flags waving a welcome. Farther out, cows freckled an open field backed by the deep, shady woods.

Indoors, the kitchen clattered with enameled plates and the crunch of sweet corn as teeth gnawed kernels of sunshine.

Tammy looked around the table. Quiet Billy, a thin teenage version of Dick, swiped at the sheen of melted butter dribbling down his chin. Floyd reached across a heaping bowl of green beans for the salt and pepper shakers while Dick stabbed his fork into another slice of ham on the platter. Mom, sturdy and comfortable like a well-used sofa, was, as usual, up and down from her chair, back and forth to the counter, refilling serving bowls, bringing another pitcher of iced tea and checking on the peach pie in the oven.

Floyd winked broadly at Dick and Billy before he turned to his daughter-in-law. "Say, Tammy. Haven't met up with any mice over at yer new place yet, have ya? Huh?"

The question brought on a gale of laughter, just as it had since last winter when she and Dick still lived here. Startled once by a mouse near the bathroom sink, she'd jumped on top of the toilet lid, screaming and hollering. Although the creature was long gone by the time the family raced to her rescue, even now Tammy shuddered at the episode, her city-girl sensibilities bruised by the experience. But every mention of the memory still tickled Dick's family and she smiled sheepishly at them as they teased her again.

Although she had appreciated Mom's hospitality before she and Dick moved out—as well as the rent-free accommodations of the drafty old farmhouse that so favorably suited their financial situation, Tammy had been eager to find a place of their own, where the haunting whistle of wind wouldn't edge their bedroom window. She craved a house. A house they could call home.

She wanted to live in a place with real streets and more people and accessible shopping within walking distance; Americans drove everywhere and she missed walking. She wanted a place where she and Dick could establish their family and live by themselves and create a nest for their new baby.

But before they could find such a place, Tammy had gone into labor January 23, 1977, on the morning of the biggest snow storm of the winter. With one eye on the slippery road and the other on his terrified wife, Dick muscled the car through thick, swirling flakes, daring to drive a hair-raising thirty miles an hour on the long ride into St. Louis.

Small, dark-headed Ginny—named Virginia Hoa Fadler, in honor of both grandmothers—was born later that evening. With a gentle finger, Tammy traced the baby's pretty round face, smoothing the mop of thick black hair and admiring tiny feet, before she nuzzled her close.

"Gin-nee," she sighed into one seashell ear.

Although she was a colicky, difficult infant, the family adored Ginny. Dick, tickled to have a daughter, doted on her; and her easy-going, unflappable sister-in-law Judy helped a lot with the baby's care. In spite of their assistance, Tammy missed too much school during the following twelve weeks—so much she could neither keep up nor catch up, overwhelmed as she was with the adjustments to new motherhood and the never-ending piles of clothes supplied by the two dry cleaners in Festus. Regretfully, she dropped her GED classes.

By the following spring, after Dick finally landed a job doing shift work for an area smelting business, the St. Joe Lead Company, Tammy persuaded him to move to a small rental on Third Street. Excited to leave the countryside and live in town, she enrolled in the Adult Continuing Education program at Jefferson College, a scant eleven miles away.

When she learned about an opening in a business downtown, she dared to apply.

To her delight, the manager at Golde's Department Store hired her to do—what else?—alterations. Gradually, Tammy noticed she no longer minded the trade she'd considered tedious, futureless and beneath her in Vietnam. In fact, she prided herself in pleasing her customers with a job well done. The people in Festus appreciated her workmanship, admiring the sewing skills she had mastered, both with needle and machine, and seemed to rely on her knowledge. Her experience. Her expertise.

Yes, she admitted with a start. *Expertise!*

By applying herself diligently, she had become an expert at something and, even more importantly, she'd learned to leverage it to her advantage. To raise her standard of living. To provide for herself and her family.

Maybe, she mused, *it isn't exactly the career I craved as a young girl, but I've certainly used it to advance my lot in life.*

Now, with more income available, Tammy set her heart and her sights on home ownership. She liked the idea of sinking money into a property rather than watching it evaporate with each month's rent.

Dick, on the other hand, was not enthusiastic about her ambitions.

One day, he found Tammy sitting cross-legged in the middle of their bed. He watched, perplexed, as she dumped a jar of hoarded pennies, nickels and dimes onto the spread, separating and counting them.

"Whatcha doin'?"

"Thih for our new how." Deftly rolling coins the way she had learned back at the NCO Club in Long Binh, Tammy didn't look up.

Dick's eyes rolled in wry amusement. "It'll take way more than that to land us in a house."

"We can do thih. It possee-ble! You see." With an index finger, she flicked fifty more dimes into a small stack that she dropped into a paper roll.

But her husband was not willing to humor her. "What's wrong with this place, anyway? You always want more." Dick threw up his hands and walked away.

Tammy counted out fifty pennies for the next roll.

Keeping track of For Sale signs and listings in the local newspaper, she sorted through available properties with the hawkish eye of a Khan Hoi housewife at a vegetable stall. After careful consideration and cautious deliberation, she chose a modest four-room on Ridge Avenue. With its bonus basement, the structure was a mansion by Vietnamese standards.

The house was listed at $18,000.

The bank requested a down payment of $1,800.

Tammy calculated her assets. After totaling the money she'd managed to put into a savings account, the $400 her sister-in-law Toni agreed to lend them and the latest batch of rolled coins, she came up with a scant $1,000.

Just do.

Ma's voice, always sensible. Ma, with her strong back and willing hands. Ma, who would do anything for the survival and future of the family she loved.

Just do.

Tammy felt a catch in her heart. She took a deep breath and decided to make an offer.

She met with the realtor.

"We will buy that how," she spoke with a measured assurance that belied her pounding heart, "ih you ask owe-er to car-ree the eigh hun-reh dollah an pay all my clo-seen fee an . . ."

She saw a doubtful expression inch across the agent's face as he gazed at the dainty foreigner in front of him. Without allowing any doubt to creep into her voice, she jutted her jaw, stood taller and plowed on. ". . . an gih me time an we sine paper an . . ."

By now, the man's eyebrows nearly touched his hairline.

". . . an I lay-er pay owe-er mon-nee due," she ended with a breathless flourish of triumph.

A long, heavy silence fell across the room as the realtor weighed her gutsy offer. He scratched his head. "Now, let me see if I understand what you're proposing, Mrs. Fadler. You want the owner to carry eight hundred dollars? *And* pay for all your closing fees, too?" He frowned at her nod. "That means you're only putting a thousand dollars down."

He examined the tips of his well-polished shoes. He stuffed his restless hands into the rear pockets of his slacks, muttering something under his breath. At last he looked up and smiled. "That's what we agents call 'creative financing,' Mrs. Fadler. You're quite the little wheeler-dealer, aren't you?" His grin broadened. "You ever think about becoming a real estate agent?"

Tammy clasped her hands, glancing away. "No. Oh, no, I dohn theen so."

They closed on the house that December.

Chapter 21

Golde's Department Store, 1980
Festus, Missouri

In Due Time

Golde's Department Store prided itself on two things: the wide array of quality goods stocked throughout and its customized service. Whether they sought glassware or gifts, shoes or sheets, patrons could be certain Golde's would meet their needs.

Situated at the Twin City Mall on Truman Boulevard, the department store kept its brick façade well scrubbed, its entry well swept and its plate glass windows well dressed, usually with an attractive, artistic display of men's, women's and children's clothing appropriate to the season.

Tammy loved her job at the high-end store. Nestled in her own cozy corner, she tackled each alteration project as it was handed to her.

"Tammy, can you shorten these pants and take in this waist?"

"Tammy, this gentleman needs the neck tightened on his shirt."

"Tammy, can you adjust these sleeves?"

Her answer was always the same measured phrase: "I am happ-ee to."

When she was asked to take up the shoulders in a men's suit, an arduous chore, she didn't cringe. Instead, she smiled. "Yes, I can do thih."

She knew she could do it, would do it. Would figure out a way to get it done. And she did.

Tammy liked her fellow employees at Golde's.

She liked the assistant manager, Ernie. She liked Betty in the rear office, Bob Russell in the warehouse, Helen over in the Children's Department, Shirley back in Draperies. In fact, she adored Shirley who had become mentor, friend and surrogate mother to the young Vietnamese woman so far from her native country and the family who, she feared, had been casualties under the Communists' régime. Furthermore, Tammy admired Mom Shirley's skill with the sewing machine and her ability to create custom drapes. No, making friends at Golde's was not hard, not hard at all.

Tammy appreciated the way she fit in at the store.

Everyone had accepted her, given her a sense of belonging since the first day she joined them. When they learned she was studying for her citizenship exam, they encouraged her. As she stumbled her way through the required reading material, they quizzed her, explaining the branches of government and simplifying the mind-numbing intricacies of the Constitution.

After she was sworn in at a solemn, 1979 ceremony, they even celebrated with her.

And, when Dick showed up at the store later that same year with a letter from Ma—at last, word from home—her dear friends at Golde's rejoiced, and cried, with her.

It had been four years, four long years since the fall of Saigon; four harrowing years without a word from her family.

Although Tammy had lost complete contact with them, she never stopped thinking about them, never stopped writing to them, never stopped enclosing small amounts of money inside every letter, even though she knew some would be opened and others stolen. She kept writing. She still kept writing.

I'm here.

Are you okay?

Enclosed is money for food. I'm sorry it isn't more.

I'm here.

Is everyone well?

Are you still there?

I'm here. I'm still here.

And now, now—a letter. An answer at last with news from home.

Tammy's hand trembled as she opened the red and blue envelope. She sucked in her breath even as her gaze raced down the page crowded with Ma's precise handwriting. They were all fine, Ma wrote, although so much had changed. It was difficult to travel outside the neighborhood with the restrictions now instituted by the Communists. Food was scarce and so were jobs. Sister Thirteen was now a big girl of seven years, Sister Five gave birth to a daughter, Brother Seven had been taken to a "re-education" camp, Ba had not been taken—yet—but was having difficulty finding any employment at all . . .

Tammy's shoulders slumped in relief as she whispered a prayer of gratitude. From Ma's stilted wording, it was obvious she couldn't talk freely and feared the letter would fall into the wrong hands. Still, they were all alive and doing well. As well as anyone could do under their circumstances. Shaking off the gloom that threatened with that thought, she turned to share the letter with her dear friends at Golde's.

Most of all, Tammy adored her boss at the classy store.

Kind-hearted Joe, with his combed brown hair and tidy suit, was a gentleman and a gentle man who always treated her well. He trusted her to do her job, never checking to see that she stayed on task, never treating her like a second-class citizen. His dry wit, warm eyes and offers to assist where he was needed made him a pleasure to work for and with, this man who himself once prayed for letters—a decade earlier—when his son Ron served in Vietnam. It wasn't long before Joe trained Tammy to help out front during the holidays, wrap gifts and clerk in both the Gifts and the Children's departments.

Less than a year after she'd started at Golde's, Tammy approached her fatherly boss with a sly grin. "Joe, I have sumfing I got to tell you."

"What's that, Tammy?"

"My rabb-it die."

"Your rabbit died? Why, I'm sorry."

Tammy scowled. "What you meen, you sor-ree?"

But Joe had already turned to his assistant manager and, with grave concern, he said, "Did you hear that, Ernie? Tammy's rabbit died."

Ernie's gaze darted between the perplexity in Tammy's face and the consternation in Joe's. He laughed. "She's just telling you she's pregnant, Joe!"

Tickled with her news, once he understood it, Joe had agreeably let her work through the entire pregnancy. He eagerly welcomed Tammy's new son when Richie—named Richard Bé to honor Dick as well as Tammy's father—arrived September 7, 1979.

No wonder it was a defining moment in Tammy's life when she received a phone call early one Saturday.

"Hello, Tammy? It's Helen."

"Hi, Helen."

"Uh, Tammy." The regret in Helen's voice was obvious. "I need to tell you something."

"Okay."

"Well, I thought you would want to know this before you come into work Monday."

Tammy wondered why Helen hesitated. "Yes?" she prompted.

"Ummm . . . Joe got fired."

"Fire?" Tammy gasped. Swallowed. Hard. "Wha you mean, Joe got fire? Wha hap-pen?"

"I'm not really sure. Mr. Golde just came in and—fired him."

"But, he goo boss. Why he geh fire?"

"I don't know, maybe they have a plan. Maybe they want to replace him for cheaper pay. Truthfully, no one is sure why it happened."

Tammy didn't know what to say, so she said nothing.

"Well . . . I just wanted you to know. So you wouldn't be surprised on Monday. Sorry to have to tell you the bad news. Bye."

Tammy stared at the wall. When she heard a loud buzzing, she stared at the receiver in her hand. At last, she returned it to its cradle. Softly. Gently.

She pulled out a chair at the kitchen table, easing herself into it.

Joe? Fired?

Likable, lovable, hard-working Joe . . . fired?

The news left her stunned.

The entire community of Festus admired Joe; everyone at Golde's loved him. He was a good boss, a good employee and he was so good at his job that . . .

His job? Why it was more than a job! Joe had been at Golde's Department Store more than two decades, the span of an entire career.

She leaned down to pick up Ginny's baby doll from the kitchen floor. Fidgeting with its clothes, she pressed each wrinkle between her fingers, smoothing and straightening. At last she set the doll aside and folded her hands in her lap, concentrating, thinking hard about Helen's news.

Joe is my superior. My boss. A fair man, highly respected by everyone.

Her thoughts stumbled, screeched to a stop.

Yet, one day he's employed, the next day, he's not.

Tammy squinted out the window.

If I put in twenty years like Joe, is that what's going to happen to me? Someone just decides to fire me one day?

She frowned, disgruntled.

There's got to be a better way.

Her fingers drummed the tabletop.

I don't want someone else to be in charge of my future, to decide whether I go or whether I stay. I don't like having someone choose whether I work or whether I'm jobless and whether I can pay my bills or whether I can't.

She planted her palms on the kitchen table, pushing back her chair with enough force to scrape the floor.

I don't know what I'll do, or how I'll do it, but from now on I'm going to work for myself.

Tammy stood, squared her shoulders and came to a firm decision.

And, if someone's ever going to fire me, it's going to be ME!

CHAPTER 22

Boatmen's Bank of Jefferson County, 1981
Festus, Missouri

Banking on It

1. Sewing
2. Alterations
3. Embroidery
4. Cleaning
5. Cooking
6. Bartending
7. Managing Inventory
8. Balancing Books

With a sweep of pencil, Tammy made a thick black line through the first three items. Even so, the length of the list impressed her. When had she gained so many marketable skills?

More importantly, what did she want to do with them?

After reassessing her list, Tammy turned in her resignation at Golde's Department Store. Although she would miss her friends there, the place felt different without Joe.

She remembered a comment he'd made one day during an afternoon coffee break.

"Do you know how to cook Chinese?"

She shook her head.

"Too bad. I love to eat Chinese food. By far, the best place I've found is Leong's Restaurant over in St. Louis." Joe had actually smacked his lips and looked heavenward. "Wow! That man can cook!"

Because of Joe's firing, Tammy knew she wanted to work for herself. Knew she needed something that would pay well, with the flexibility to continue her schooling and spend time with her children. She wanted to work in Festus and she knew there was not a Chinese restaurant in town. She understood the food industry top to bottom, from managing the business side to waiting and bussing tables. And, thanks to Ma and the fine chefs who had trained her at MAC-V and Long Binh, she was accomplished in both Vietnamese and American cuisine.

Now, she took a deep breath at the thought, what if she learned to cook Chinese?

She landed a new job. At Leong's Restaurant in St. Louis, learning from the best. Learning from the master. It was an—apprenticeship of sorts. Only she chose not to mention that fact to Mr. Leong.

Between them, Dick and Judy managed to care for Ginny and Richie while Tammy worked six days a week from 10 a.m.

to 10 p.m., temporarily trading her continuing-education classes for a different kind of learning. Always a diligent employee, she kept a watchful eye on the machinations of Mr. Leong's profitable venture, determined to absorb whatever it took to duplicate his success.

"*Có khó mới có miếng ăn,*" Tammy muttered as she drove home one night, utterly exhausted. *No sweet without sweat.*

After commuting the sixty miles to Leong's Restaurant for six months, Tammy quit, comfortable with the new knowledge and skills she'd gained. Meanwhile, she listened to friends and neighbors, clerks at the grocery store. She questioned teachers, tutors and classmates in her continuing-education classes at Jefferson College. She watched and waited; she looked and learned.

Until she found it: The Flamingo Café.

Situated across the street from Jefferson Memorial Hospital, the homey eatery boasted an all-American menu and a regular clientele of medical staff and area residents. She heard that the owners, Clyde and Bonnie Hawkins, who were dealing with a health crisis, had decided to sell, to retire. The price tag for the business was a hefty $12,000. The rental of the building itself would need to be renegotiated.

Tammy calculated the feasibility, thought through the risk, dreamed about the potential. It offered everything she needed. All that she wanted.

Could she?

Was it possible for a little Vietnamese woman with no money and only a fifth-grade education to purchase and operate a restaurant, by herself—on her own—in this country that offered so many options?

Did she dare even try?

With her heart pounding, Tammy approached the lenders at Commerce Bank in Festus, where she was handed a detailed application to complete. An anxious two weeks later, she received a letter in the mail: LOAN REQUEST DENIED.

With her heart racing, Tammy approached the lenders at Crystal City State Bank, where she was handed a detailed application to complete. An angst-filled two weeks later, she received a letter in the mail: LOAN REQUEST DENIED.

Both letters mentioned the high risk of the restaurant business. Risky? Tammy shrugged. She knew what she was doing. She knew how to do it and do it well. What risk?

Both letters mentioned her lack of capital. They meant that she had no money.

"If I got mon-nee, why I nee dem? If I got mon-nee, why I ask mohr?" She shook her head over the enigma of American lending institutions.

With her jaw jutted and her lips pressed in a thin line, Tammy drove to nearby Pevely and stood on the sidewalk, cocking her head to look up at the sign: Boatmen's Bank of Jefferson County.

I just need enough money so I can buy the restaurant. Other people do this, I can, too. I know I can.

Tammy smoothed her hair, charged inside and marched to the loan desk.

"I lie tawk sum one abou a low."

The receptionist smiled. "And what type of loan are you interested in?"

"Smahl beez-nuss."

"You'll need to fill out an application. Here are the papers . . ."

"No." Tammy shook her head firmly. "No. I wohn fill out. I wan tawk sum bod-ee."

"I see." The woman's brows arched. "Well, then, you'll need to talk to our Vice President, Mr. Dietsch. Lee Dietsch. Let me show you into his office."

After short introductions, Tammy was seated in front of his imposing oak desk. She explained her desire to buy The Flamingo Café, repeating her request to apply for a small-business loan.

"Here are the forms." The thin, hawkish man held out an application packet. "Now," he dismissed her, "why don't you take this home with you. You can fill it out and mail it to us late . . ."

"Stop!" Flinging an open palm against his words, Tammy stood and looked the startled banker straight in the eye.

"Look, I feel so min-nee thih piece pa-per an I know wha go-een to hap-pen when I lee heer—two wik you sin me led-der say-een 'No'! So you not go-een to gih me mon-nee like the ress of them dohn, tell me now and save you stam and save me fill out thih piece pa-per."

She stretched to her full height, planting her palms on her hips. "I dohn nee two wik fine out. Y-you tell me 'no' to-day!"

Mr. Dietsch ran his fingers through his peppered hair. Sliding narrow glasses to the tip of his nose, he looked over the top, eyes crinkled, kindly and calm.

"Now, now young lady, why don't you sit back down." His voice was steady, serene. "How about coffee? Could I get you a cup of coffee?"

Tammy knew he saw the desperation on her face, knew he heard the anguish in her voice. She gulped for air, sinking back into the office chair. "Yes, yes. Coff-ee."

She summoned a last trace of bravado, speaking to his back as he exited the office. "An I wan creem my coff-ee."

The loan officer returned with a steaming mug and placed it on his desk. "Is this enough cream?"

Tammy stared into the swirled coffee. Picking it up, she nodded. Sipped. Nodded again.

"Well, now, Mrs. Fadler." Resting his elbows on the arms of his chair, the banker steepled his fingers and smiled. "Tell me about this business you hope to buy. Why, exactly, do you want to operate a restaurant?"

Tammy knew she should tell him about her desire for independence, her worries since her boss was fired, her need to feel secure.

"I wan breen my fam-lee heer."

There. She'd said it aloud. And no one was more surprised than she was. She had harbored the secret desire within her heart—unspoken—where it simmered, first as a mere thought to mull over, then as a need so strong it burned. Tammy's eyes welled with tears, in spite of her earlier spunk.

"Ma . . . Ba . . ." Her words stumbled, tripping over each other like newly released captives running for freedom.

The increasing dangers, the deaths, the . . . the . . . murders under Communism. The deteriorating lack of commodities, jobs and money in Saigon. Ma, trying her best to feed the thirteen siblings Tammy had left behind. Ba, in danger of imprisonment, or worse, because of a job he'd once held at the court house. Brother Seven, wasting away—or was he already dead?—in a re-education camp. Xuan, petite Sister Five, three inches shy of five foot, laboring at the cargo port, her back bent like a bamboo pole, as she carried forty-nine kilo bags of rice onto the loading dock. All day. Every day. Just to survive.

Feeling an enduring ache in her own spine that resulted from toting buckets of water as a child, Tammy caught her breath on a sob. She wanted so much more for her sister. A better life for them all.

Mr. Dietsch, she suddenly realized, had listened intently to her spate, never interrupting, letting her spew on and on and on. In English? Vietnamese? She looked into his eyes, not certain how much of her galloping thoughts she'd actually been able to express. Enough, apparently. She could read his emotion, sense his compassion.

She sniffled.

He handed her a tissue.

Tammy mopped her face. "I heer so min-ee year, mak-een mon-nee day and nigh. But not e-nuff. Never not e-nuff."

He waited until she composed herself.

"Where did you learn to cook? What kind of experience do you have in the restaurant business?"

Tammy told him about the chefs she'd trained under in Vietnam, her jobs with the United States military, working in Fort Meade and under Mr. Leong.

"I can do thih. I har wor-ker. I will-een pay price. You give me chance, I can do."

"I tell you what. Why don't you go home and call me later today?"

"Wha time to-day?"

"After lunch." He accompanied her to the door of his office. "I'll have an answer for you then."

Hardly daring to hope, Tammy sat in her kitchen and watched the second hand crawl from number to number. At precisely 1:00 p.m., she placed her call.

"Can you come back in?" asked Mr. Dietsch. "I'd like to talk with you."

This time, the receptionist merely nodded her through to his office.

"Well, young lady, let's cut right to the chase. I have no idea why I'm doing this, but I've got a feeling I can count on you. I had a talk with our bank president, John Lanham, and explained your situation." He locked his fingers behind his head and leaned back in his chair, his elbows bent like the wings of chim sac birds, ready to take flight.

Tammy held her breath, waiting for his next words.

"We decided to give you the money."

Tammy gripped the edge of her chair, not certain she understood. "A low? You shure a low? You make me the smahl beez-nuss low?"

The banker nodded, leaning forward. "The loan is yours. Now, don't disappoint me."

Tammy shook her head. "I wohn!" She reached for his hand, pumping it. "Oh, no, I shure wohn! I will pay bac, you see!"

Laughing, he squeezed her fingers before pulling his own from her enthusiastic, and surprisingly strong, grip.

"A low. A low. I get smahl beez-nuss low!" Tammy sang under her breath as she turned to walk away.

"Uh, Mrs. Fadler?"

She paused at the door.

"Just as a small favor to me—and Boatmen's Bank," he winked and handed her a sheaf of papers, "would you mind filling out this application for a loan?"

A mere two weeks later, Tammy received a formal letter in the mail.

LOAN REQUEST APPROVED.

CHAPTER 23

Jefferson College, 1985
Festus, Missouri

Business and More

Business was brisk at The Saigon Restaurant. Customers still ordered American hamburgers with a side of fries or biscuits with gravy, but many others came in for chow mein and fried won ton. The skills she had honed under Mr. Leong's tutelage paid off: Tammy introduced a complete menu of the Chinese fare she'd mastered, adding her signature Vietnamese flavor. It was one way she justified the sentimental name she'd chosen.

Her budget too tight to do much more, Tammy placed only a few small ads in area newspapers. Even so, as word spread about the tasty Asian cuisine, the clientele grew. Tammy's work hours expanded, as well, starting in the yawning blackness of pre-dawn for the breakfast crowd and ending when the last customers wandered home from the after-midnight meal she offered for weekend dancers who frequented her establishment.

"You can do this," Dick encouraged as his bone-weary wife stumbled to bed.

Unusually supportive of her newest endeavor, he helped with the children, shuttling them between babysitters, school and the restaurant. When he stopped by the restaurant, he made himself useful, lugging heavy supplies, hauling out trash, making coffee, serving customers and working the cash register.

When it came time to renew the three-year building lease, business was steady enough that Tammy opted out in favor of a newer, bigger location she rented on Kenner Street with the blessings of Boatmen's Bank.

And Lee Dietsch.

Over the past few years, Lee had taken a personal interest in Tammy, mentoring her along the road to success. She sometimes stopped at the bank to ask him questions over a cup of coffee—with cream, please. Thanks to his explanations and warnings, she had avoided the assumption of vendor liabilities, learned how to negotiate payments and how to charge and to figure discounts. She looked forward to each of his casual visits at her restaurant, eager to discuss ideas for the new kitchen she was planning or the updated lighting she'd selected or the used bar she'd nabbed at auction. Delighted, she noticed that he, like her other customers, favored the Chinese food offered on her menu.

Tammy marveled at the ready acceptance she felt from the community. Lee, all her customers at The Saigon Restaurant, her coworkers at Golde's and the patrons at the dry cleaners, her teachers and tutors and the new friends she'd made on campus. Everyone seemed to embrace her openly, in spite of her connections to the controversial Vietnam War.

Of course, there was one unfortunate incident, the very first year she had opened the restaurant. As she had exited the kitchen to visit with her customers out front, a man caught sight of her.

Obviously intoxicated, he reeled his way across the room, screaming at her, his words slurred, but his hatred obvious. "Why you little *****! I oughta schtring ya up and hang ya from the ceiling, ya no good *****!"

The Vietnam veteran ranted his hatred of the unholy war that stole his youth and killed his friends. Of the government that sent them there, to a godforsaken country nobody ever even heard of, where you couldn't tell the enemy from those that you might dare to trust.

"And you—you little *****! Why I'm gonna take you and . . ."

He kept ranting while they phoned the police, and he was still hurtling sordid obscenities and haunting threats when he was escorted out.

Shaken and trembling, Tammy fumbled for a chair.

Oddly, it wasn't the soldier or his ravings that disturbed her. She'd dealt with her share of distraught GIs at the Army base in Long Binh. She recognized in this man the same underlying vulnerability she'd witnessed in other soldiers who had faced the atrocities of battle. She understood the crippling pain that fueled his rage.

What she hadn't expected was the depth of agitation she saw in him more than a decade after the war was over. His emotions were still raw, still open, still bleeding. Proof that the war hadn't ended in Saigon. Not for him. Not for her.

✦ ✦ ✦

Sidetracked with her young family and her galloping new business, Tammy had let her adult education classes lapse, but not her hunger for knowledge. She missed everything about school. The books. The teachers. The learning. Rather than return to her tutors, perhaps it was time to set her sights even higher?

Tammy decided to go to college.

She stepped into the Registrar Office at Jefferson.

"I wan to sigh up class," she told the receptionist.

"Why, certainly. Let's see, here's some literature you'll want to read, brochures, a catalog listing the courses we offer." The woman slid an official form across the counter. "And you'll need to fill this out."

"Than you." Tammy scooted everything into a tidy stack and turned to leave.

"Oh, and, miss? You'll need to bring in or mail us your high-school transcript before we can process your application."

Tammy's neck stiffened slightly. A faint queasiness rolled in her stomach. She hadn't realized there would be a requirement like that. After all, when she attended the continuing education classes here, no one asked her for a transcript or questioned the GED test she'd never bothered to take. But now, now?

Tammy clutched the precious pile of papers to her chest and paused to mull the situation, considering her options. She realized her fifth-grade education was not enough to qualify for acceptance, but she just knew she could manage college classes if only she had the chance. She simply could not let this opportunity slip through her fingers.

Yet, she didn't want to lie.

"High skoo tra-scrip?" Tammy leaned forward slightly, tilting her chin and frowning, to point out the obvious. "But I . . . I from Vietnam. Sow Vietnam." She kept her face open, frank.

There. I didn't lie—I just didn't tell.

After all, it was general knowledge that the Communists ruled her homeland, and it would be logical that a corrupt government would not relinquish school records of any South Vietnamese expatriate.

"Oh, yes, yes, of course you wouldn't have your high school transcript." The receptionist readily made the assumption Tammy had hoped for, her voice soothing and sympathetic. "Well, honey, I'm not sure just how to handle this. Let me see what I can do."

She slipped from the room but returned shortly.

"We think we can make an exception to the rule in your case. You just go ahead and fill out those forms and return them before the deadline. Do you need any help?"

Tammy shook her head, trying to temper her elation into a grateful smile rather than the gloating grin that threatened to erupt.

Later, her glee evolved into amazement when, as a non-traditional student, she was offered grant money to offset childcare, tuition and fees—as long as she carried the required minimum hours each semester.

"No pro-blem. I can do thih!" she reassured her counselor and the helpful registrar staff.

Amazing! she thought. *Such unimaginable opportunity in America. I cannot believe the school is so generous here, so good here. Back home, I worked hard to go to school. Yet, all you have to do here to take advantage of the education system is show up. And you don't even need money. They actually* pay *you to go to school! How can this be?*

But adding college courses to her hectic routine made her schedule even more complicated. It was a delicate balancing act, to do all and be all.

Tammy kept her business open seven days a week, which meant she showed up at 4:30 every morning to prepare for the 6:00 breakfast crowd. At 7:20 on weekdays, she raced to Jefferson College in time for her 7:45 a.m. class, then back to The Saigon Restaurant for the customers who arrived at 11:00 for lunch. Afternoons allowed her a few hours of break to do her homework and play with Ginny and Richie, who were growing up, Vietnamese style, around her feet at the restaurant. Only after the kitchen was cleaned to her satisfaction, the toilet scrubbed spotless and the floors swept out front did she traipse home, usually around 9:00 at night—except on weekends, of course, when she didn't close until 2:30 a.m.

Even so, Fortune smiled and Tammy was grateful.

Her health was excellent. Her young children were thriving. She had an able staff of two cooks and three waitresses she'd inherited with her purchase of the Flamingo Café. And when Kim Nguyen, a recent refugee from North Vietnam, arrived in Festus, Tammy hired her, too.

Speaking their native tongue brought joy and comfort to both women. The syllables flowed with memories of rice paddies and pagodas, the squall of seagulls and the grit of sand-baked toes.

The only flaw in Tammy's life was her husband.

As her schedule revved up, Dick—once so supportive and helpful—griped about the hours she kept. Complained when she enrolled in college. Fretted about her time away from family and home, upset at the energy and effort she poured into The Saigon.

And then he wasn't talking much at all. He disappeared into his shell, a turtle protecting his soft underbelly.

Tammy knew they were drifting apart, already had drifted apart, had grown in opposite directions. Understanding that she was no longer the kind of wife Dick wanted her to be, she also knew there was no going back. She had worked hard for her achievements.

She had a future to see to, full of goals, plans and dreams. They all included hard work and, above all, an education.

Tammy and Dick filed for divorce.

CHAPTER 24

Jefferson College Library, circa 1980s
Festus, Missouri

E-I, I-E–Ohhh!

A frown creased Tammy's forehead.

Raking her fingers through her shiny mane, she tilted her head back and stared blankly at the acoustical tiles checkering the library ceiling.

A huge sigh exploded from her lips. She adored school, adored everything about it: the act of learning, the environment and the new friends she'd made. She felt comfortable in the classroom setting, even though she struggled with the language. Still, she understood the need to build a better foundation by studying the elements of spelling and grammar. At the Learning Center, she'd received a textbook, *English 2600*, for that purpose.

Tackling any foreign language, of course, was daunting. But English seemed especially complex—impossible even—with all its regulations and restrictions. Like the line she'd just memorized: "Use *I* before *E*—except after *C*."

Tracing the lines with her finger, she scanned the page until she found the sentence again. She read on.

"There is another exception to this rule. When the vowels sound like *A* as in *weight* and *neighbor*, use *E* before *I*."

"Rules, rules, rules," she muttered under her breath. "Why so min rules? Spe-slee when dey goin to breck dem!"

Her eyes widened as she continued to the end of the paragraph.

"An additional exception occurs when we use *E* before *I* in words such as *their* and *heir*."

Well! Exasperation choked her. *Apparently, there can even be an exception to the exception to the exception!*

Tammy grimaced.

Nothing about this foreign language was simple or clear cut, and Americans chose to complicate it even more by inventing words—all with individual meanings—that sounded the same but were spelled differently. She looked at the paper provided by her tutor.

aisle – isle
all – awl
altar – alter
arc – ark
aught – ought
bail – bale
ball – bawl

Tammy skimmed through the alphabetized list.

flew – flue
holy – wholly
jam – jamb

That's jamb with a silent B, she interjected with a tinge of pride.

mantle – mantel
principal – principle
rough – ruff
stationary – stationery

And here? Yet more words, these in groups of three. Three!

cent – scent – sent
cite – sight – site
pair – pare – pear
rain – rein – reign

She reread the last entry with its *rein* and *reign*, immediately recognizing one of those dreadful exceptions to the fussy Rule of *EI-IE*—because the vowels sound like *A*. Tammy shuddered.

slew – slue – slough
to – too – two

She screeched to a halt at the next entry, stunned. She counted. One. Two. Three. Four. Four? Really, four words?

right – rite – wright – write

"An all soun sam?" she wondered. Embarrassed when she realized she'd spoken aloud, Tammy glanced around the library to see if anyone had heard her. Then, with deliberation, she pointed at the words. One. By. One.

right
rite
wright
write

And she whispered them, individually. Just to see if it was really possible.

"Rye."

"Rye."

"Rye."

"Rye."

Tammy nodded. Satisfied. Indeed, they *did* all sound the same!

Settling back into her chair, she shuffled a pile of papers until she came to the other list she'd been given, this one a compilation of words with identical spellings but different meanings. *And* different pronunciations. Thankfully, these examples were used in sentences. Maybe she could decipher them without asking for help. She started reading.

The *invalid* knew her prescription was *invalid.*
He wanted to *project* the *project* onto the screen.
The *dove dove* into the sea.
She paused at the *entrance* to *entrance* him.
He was not *present* to *present* his findings.

Puzzled, she paused and returned to reread the directions at the top of the page. Yes, yes, she'd understood them correctly the first time. These were, indeed, words spelled the same that did not sound the same.

They can't be serious about this, she thought. *What do they mean that the words don't sound the same? The same as what?*

And, anyway, how could she be expected to pronounce them differently when she didn't know what "different" was? Different from . . . what?

This was much, much, much too much for a tiny, uneducated Vietnamese girl to comprehend. Just when she thought she had something figured out, the pattern changed. Those awful exceptions reared their gruff heads to roar in defiance. She closed her eyes and shook her own head to clear her brain. But, like a persistent reel of film, those complex grammar rules—along with the odd exceptions and the tangled breaks in pattern that she had studied with such diligence—scrolled relentlessly, tirelessly through her mind.

Singular and Plural
one tree – two trees
one deer – two deer
one leaf – two leaves
one foot – two feet

Tenses
come – came – come
drink – drank – drunk
go – went – gone

lay – laying – laid – laid
lie – lying – lay – lain

Contractions
I + am = I'm
you + are = you're
she + is = she's
he + had = he'd
they + have = they've

Personal Pronouns
I – my, mine – me
you – your, yours – you
she – her, hers – her
he – his – him
it – its – it

Behind her weary eyelids, the film gained even more momentum until it sped, bled and blurred.

Modifiers
Compound Objects
FiguresofSpeechFiniteVerbs
GenderPossessivesAbbreviationsAdjec
tivesPunctuationCapitalizationAdverbsClauses
AbnormalVerbsModifiersParticiplesvowelsinfinitivespronounsan
tecedentsconjugaaaaa . . .

Dazed, Tammy groaned. And, just to be dramatic, she groaned one more time—before she swept back her stack of precious books to teeter at the very edge of the library table and buried her head in her arms.

Chapter 25

The Saigon Restaurant, 1987
Festus, Missouri

On Fire

College assignments. Single parenting. Long work hours at The Saigon Restaurant.

Driven by the subtle heartbeat of restaurateuring, Tammy discovered a measure of satisfaction in the rhythm of her full days, feeling her life settle into peaceful harmony. She and Dick were amicable; the kids well adjusted, with two involved parents; her homework manageable; the business solid.

Fueled by success, she tackled each project with vigor, hardly knowing and certainly not caring that the load was heavy, that she existed on so little sleep—who had hours to loll in bed, anyway?—or that she had neither the time nor means to relax, to play or to travel.

Tammy focused fully on her dual dreams of education and financial independence. Depending on the workload of the classes, she carried three, six or sometimes nine credit hours each semester at Jefferson. Patronage at her restaurant continued to grow, bringing her a fairly reliable income, income that ensured the future of Ma, Ba, and the slew of sisters and brothers she tried so desperately to keep track of through the sporadic letters they mailed back and forth.

Family remained of utmost importance, and she wanted to rescue hers from the ever-worsening conditions in Vietnam. She wanted to bring them here, to America, to a place that Communism, war and want couldn't reach.

Paperwork.

A sigh muscled its way from Tammy's chest and exploded in the quiet of her bedroom.

Paperwork, paperwork and more paperwork.

She flicked off the lamp and tucked the blanket beneath her chin as she stared into the darkness.

Sponsoring family members was no simple chore. In order to apply, she filed detailed forms which had to meet the demands of the government. But, just as so often in the past, Fortune smiled on her once more. Thankfully, her thriving restaurant proved its value in her endeavor: It showed ownership, stability and capability. The established business indicated to authorities that she was able to support her family and that no one she brought to this country would go on welfare to burden the American people or be a liability to this land she now called Home.

Pleased with the direction and progress in her life, Tammy snuggled deeper into the bed and closed her eyes.

RRRRRING!

Her face burrowed in the pillow, Tammy reached blindly for the nightstand.

RRRRRING!

She fumbled for the phone.

RRRRRING!

"-llo." She cleared her throat. "He-llo."

"Tammy? Tammy Fadler?"

"Yes?" The glowing hands of the alarm clock pointed accusingly. It was 3:34 a.m.

"Tammy, you need to get to the restaurant. *Now,*" urged the man at the other end.

"Why? Wha wrong? Who thih?" She threw back the blankets, already reaching for the black slacks she'd worn earlier that night.

"I'm calling from the police station. There's been a fire at your place."

"No!" She tossed her head to clear it. "No!"

"Get dressed and get there as quick as you can."

Tammy finished yanking a crumpled red blouse over her head, grabbed her keys and jumped in the car.

Impossible, she assured herself. *It's not The Saigon Restaurant, not my restaurant. It can't be. He's mistaken. He's wrong. He's wrong, wrong, wrong.*

But icy fingers of fear clutched her heart, the same heart that understood, with a certainty, that policemen didn't make mistakes of that magnitude.

The scene on Kenner Street struck an odd chord. No fire kindled on the horizon. No blaze lit the landscape. No tongues of flame licked the night sky. Instead, headlights of fire trucks, police cars and other emergency vehicles pierced the darkness like the wary eyes of beasts cloaked by the jungle.

Tammy stared at the building that squatted beside the parking lot crowded with milling people.

This can't be happening to my restaurant. It just can't be.

She shook her head in firm denial and rubbed her face where she felt the marks of her pillow still creasing her cheek. She pulled her hand back, startled at the moisture on her fingertips.

Her restaurant gazed back, tears dripping freely from its shattered windows, apologetic and ashamed of the smoke it belched from a gaping, wounded mouth. Through its broken doorway, Tammy saw a trace of embers pulsing like a weak heart.

Decisively, she turned to a fireman. "It ar-righ I go in?"

"Sure, if you can handle the stink. The fire was contained to the ceiling. But I'll need to go with you. Watch out, though, it's pretty wet and warm in there." He grabbed her arm to help her across the threshold. "Careful, there, Tammy."

A quick glance told her there wouldn't be much to salvage. Her stunned gaze slowed to inspect the sight. Water dripped from the blackened ceiling onto . . . everything. A stream of shimmering shards led from the ledge of goblets and glasses. She took a mincing few steps to avoid a particularly large puddle and tried to take in the extent of the damage.

Charred woodwork framed broken dishes and splintered glassware. Tables were warped and chair seats melted. Plastic serving ware, softened by the heat, flowed into grotesque shapes.

"No-o-o-o!" The forceful moan pushed its way from the depths of her. She squeezed her eyes shut against the disaster, praying it wasn't so. Praying this was all a horrible nightmare. That she would open her eyes and find herself still tucked in bed. Warm, safe, shielded from this, this . . .

Tammy opened her eyes—to the reality of ruin.

Everything, *everything* was a mess. A huge mess. Although the fire had been contained to the fourteen-foot ceiling, what the heat and smoke hadn't ruined, the water and force of the hoses had definitely finished off.

And that acrid stench that was stinging her eyes and burning her nose and scouring the back of her throat? What was it, that smell? She'd known it once before, hadn't she?

Tammy flattened her palm against the sudden, sharp ache in her chest, surprised to feel a fresh wash of tears on her face, startled at the vivid image crowding her mind, a memory dredged from the dark past.

How old had she been? Eleven? Twelve?

And, why had she been there, at that place, at that scene, at that time?

Fate, she determined. Only Fate, and an errand for Má, perhaps, could have put her so many blocks from the marketplace in Khánh Hội. No matter the reason, she'd found herself strolling the serpentine streets of Sài Gòn that steamy June afternoon. At first, she didn't give a thought to the stream of gray-clad nuns sweeping past her until she noticed the monks in their orange robes and, taking the lead, an automobile filled with more monks.

"A parade!"

Thrilled at her good fortune, Tammy stopped at a storefront to watch.

But the car only went as far as the corner, where it stopped. The monks got out and lifted the hood. Engine trouble?

She saw the procession part around the car, stop and form a deep circle. Tammy edged closer when the monks began a solemn, rhythmic chant. Vaguely disturbed at the mournful intonation, she edged her way through the crowd that was starting to gather, until she could squeeze close enough to satisfy her curiosity.

An old Buddhist monk with shaven head and peaceful eyes sat in the middle of the city intersection, folded into a classic lotus position, fixed in sacred meditation, prayer beads in his hand. Tammy's gaze swung to the left when the nun nearest broke the cadence of her chant with a sob. Other nuns, too, began to weep.

Tammy frowned. This was nothing like the colorful, joyous parades she attended with Ba and Má. Just as she turned to push her way out of the throng, she saw a monk pouring a can of water on the meditating Buddhist, soaking his robes until a puddle of water formed around him.

She sniffed. No, no, she shook her head, not water. The oily smell penetrating the air reminded her of the navy ships at the docks where Ba worked. That large can held *gasoline*. Her eyes widened just as the aged monk struck a match.

Whoosh!

Flames and thick black smoke engulfed him, hid him from view.

The chanting stopped. No one uttered a sound. Not even the burning monk.

Tammy's jaw dropped. She didn't blink. She couldn't.

Amidst the devouring flames, the old monk's skin shriveled and melted until, in an amazingly short time, his fully charred body sat, composed, even in death—in sharp contrast to people wailing around him, their high keens mixing with the acrid stench of flesh and fuel.

Tammy's throat ached. Her nose stung and her eyes watered. She shoved her way through the crowd, stumbling across the sidewalk, praying for enough air to clear her mind of a sight so unimaginable. Gasping for enough air to cleanse her lungs of an odor so unforgettable.

So unforgettable, so unimaginable, she had forgotten she'd ever witnessed it. Until now.

Now.

When the screeching specters of Tết, too, unexpectedly arose from the past to expel their sour breath on the monk's blackened bones.

Now.

When they turned their fury on her, their fiery fingers encircling her throat.

Squeezing the life from her.

Sucking the breath from her.

Tammy stumbled from the scorched ruins of her restaurant, gulping the night air.

CHAPTER 26

Records Center, 1987–88
St. Louis, Missouri

Finding the Pearl

It was over, gone. Her precious restaurant, her livelihood, income and hope for the future. All gone.

The weeks following the fire had been a nightmare of cleanup.

"We can sa-vage thih," she muttered as employees, friends and clients helped her sort the mangled mess. She pointed at a tea cup. "We can sa-vage thah."

When she stooped to pick it up, she noticed a crack down the side. Tammy grimaced, tossing it among the other discards in the heaping Dumpster.

She often thought it would have been simpler if the building, which she didn't own, had burned completely to the ground. Instead, they all worked their way through the wreckage, a little at a time.

Tammy used her storage unit to hold the bar from the restaurant, remarkably undamaged, and any other odds and ends worth keeping. Several tables. A few chairs. Stainless-steel appliances. To her surprise, she discovered the money from that last night of business still in the drawer, intact, not even singed. And, on a shelf, her college textbooks, unharmed. Both were bright spots amid the ashes.

But the one thing, the most important thing, she couldn't salvage was her dream of reuniting her family. Without The Saigon Restaurant, she couldn't show the stability so vital to the sponsorship process. Tammy blinked back ever-present tears, afraid that if she let them fall again, the torrent might sweep her away.

Maybe that wouldn't be so bad, she thought.

She imagined a monsoon of tears sweeping her out to sea, rocking her to sleep on the waves, and carrying her safely to shore and into the arms of Ba and Ma who would welcome her with joyous laughter and pull her back into the bosom of her family who would gather for a celebration and Sister Five who would lift her laughing eyes and the others . . .

Her family.

The fantasy screeched to a halt.

And maybe that's not so bad, either, she decided. If she had set the goal once, she could certainly set it again. She focused deep inside herself, fanning the tiny ember of determination still glowing there.

But, oh, the barriers she faced with the insurance company as the agent assessed the damage to determine what her meager policy would cover. Which wasn't much. Thank goodness she'd already paid off her loan with Boatmen's Bank. She could hold her head high.

Yet it insisted on drooping, weighted by the knowledge that there wasn't enough insurance money to get the business up and running again. Months passed before she was able to collect. Meanwhile, she dealt with the headaches of yet more paperwork, all the claims and adjustments and the final, searing pangs of closing out the books to her beloved business.

Night fell like a shroud over The Saigon.

Even during those wrenching months of heartache and disappointment, Tammy had searched for a new path to continue her journey. While still keeping up her college classes, she looked for work, a way to support herself, Ginny and Richie.

Capitalizing on her past experience with the United States government, Tammy landed a Civil Service job at the Records Center in St. Louis. She spent her days pulling records for the I.R.S. and ferreting out discrepancies.

She hated her job.

The work was tedious. Boring. She disliked the routine of it almost as much as she despised the long commute from Festus to St. Louis that stole more than an hour from her schedule each morning and evening, keeping her from her children, making her late to her night classes and delaying her homework.

Her schedule was insane as she tried to be all and do all. Room Mother at her kids' school. Last week a field trip, next week a Valentine's party. Dick wasn't as readily able to help with Ginny and Richie; his new tech-support job with Motorola kept him on the road. Although she found someone to shuttle her kids to and from school and managed to arrange their after-school supervision, Tammy regretted every minute she spent away from the children.

When I had the restaurant, she remembered, *they played at my feet. I saw Richie and Ginny all the time.*

When I had the restaurant, she recalled, I *decided the schedules.* I *determined the hours apart.*

When I had The Saigon, she sighed, I *was The Boss.*

And that was it, she knew. That was the grit that irritated the oyster.

She wasn't pleased with her job at the Records Center because she preferred to work for herself. She had liked being her own master and she wanted to be her own boss again. She wanted it fiercely.

As she processed papers that day, her probing mind jumped from one career possibility to another, exploring the advantages before scrutinizing the disadvantages of every suggestion friends and acquaintances had tossed her way.

And then she found it! The idea tumbled around her mind throughout the long afternoon until at last it was polished, as smooth as a pearl.

She would become a real estate agent. Yes, she decided, that's what she would do. As an agent, she could work locally instead of wasting time on a commute. She could be there for her children. She could set her own hours and schedule her days to suit the routine of her family. And she could work with clients, real people, instead of lifeless records.

After she tucked Ginny and Richie into bed that night, Tammy sat down with the Festus Phone Book, the first step toward her new career. A friend had explained that she would need to find a broker to sponsor her through the initial schooling. Tammy wasted no time.

"Ree-a-stay," she mumbled under her breath, letting her fingers "do the walking" through the Yellow Pages like the television commercial urged.

She did her homework. She learned which realty company was selling locally, who was doing the most business.

"Thah who I wan wor for. Thah who I wan assosi-ate wih."

She found three agencies in the area—Laiben Real Estate, Empire Real Estate and Century 21 Showcase—and methodically wrote down each address.

The first broker was kind, if blunt, at her interview.

"This business is complicated. You know, the, uh, the legal side of things. You don't just walk in and start selling, you know." She saw Frank's discomfort in his eyes. They shifted from her to the window, to a thirsty potted plant, and back to her again. "I'm sorry, but I just don't think you, uh, have what it takes to succeed."

Tammy didn't comment. She clenched her hands to stop the trembling.

"And, uh, clients would find it pretty difficult to understand you." He fiddled with the slim ink pen on his desk top. "It's your English, you know? It's, uh, well, it's just not good enough."

He never returned any of her follow-up phone calls.

Crushed, she fought through her disappointment.

But I can do this. I know *I can do this.*

The second broker didn't mince words.

"Sorry," he said, the word as terse as the voice behind it. "We don't need anyone."

Tammy didn't believe him, but she nodded and left.

Oddly, she found herself thinking about the American fairy tale, "Goldilocks and the Three Bears." *Too hot, too cold;*

too hard, too soft; too big, too small. Her thoughts were glum and so was her attitude. *Will I ever find the sponsor that's just right?* She decided to make one more attempt.

The third broker greeted her with a smile.

"So, tell me what I can do for you, Mrs. Fadler. Are you buying? Selling?"

The well-groomed woman listened closely as Tammy expressed her desire to establish a new career in real estate. But Tammy noticed how her face tightened.

Shirley Overberg rested her elbows on the shiny desk and leaned forward. "And why, exactly, did you choose this business? Why, exactly, do you want to become an agent?"

Tammy listed her reasons, especially the appeal of flexible hours and being in control of her schedule so that she could spend time with Richie and Ginny and be there for them during the hours they weren't in school.

"Ah. I see." Her eyes were shuttered.

"I can do thih. I know I can do thih." Tammy's feet were planted to the floor, her fingers laced, almost prayerfully. "I ohn-lee nee a spon-ser."

Shirley sat back in the deep, upholstered swivel chair and stared doubtfully at the young woman sitting across from her. "Well, okay, okay then." She nibbled on her lower lip. "Here's how our program works. Our agency will provide you with a hundred-dollar scholarship . . ."

Tammy straightened in her seat.

". . . but you'll need to pay the rest . . ."

Tammy's head bobbed in agreement. There was just enough insurance money left to cover the rest of the tuition.

". . . then you'll attend Real Estate School for a couple of weeks."

Tammy knew it would take longer, twice as long, because she would need to register for night sessions rather than the more-compact day sessions. She couldn't afford to miss a single paycheck from the Records Center.

"At the end of the class, you'll take a test . . ."

Tammy didn't even cringe. Instead, blood coursed through her veins in welcome anticipation. A new opportunity to study. Another chance to learn!

". . . and if you pass the test . . ."

Of course she would pass!

". . . *if* and *when* you pass the test . . . well, then, you come back here to see me when you get the results. We'll talk some more at that time, and I'll tell you what happens next. But, I warn you, real estate is full of challenges."

Challenges? Now that was a word Tammy understood in any language. Challenges, she could handle. Mentally, she rolled up her sleeves, ready to meet the dare.

Shirley stood and came around the desk, her hand extended. "How does that sound to you? Do we have a deal?"

Tammy jumped to her feet, knowing she wore a foolish grin and not caring in the least. "Oh shure, shure, it a deel!"

And so began a new routine. For the next month, Tammy spent her days slogging through records for the I.R.S. On her way home from work each evening, she put in several more hours at Real Estate School. Over the weekends, she spent time with Ginny and Richie. And she studied.

Three weeks after she took the real estate exam, Tammy strode into Shirley's office and slapped the results letter onto her desk.

"I pass!" she bragged. "In one try ohn-lee, I pass!"

Shirley's tidy brows shot up. "I . . . see." She picked up the certificate and read it, read it slowly, thoroughly, line by line. "So you did, Tammy, so you did. You passed after all."

After all? Didn't she expect me to pass?

Shirley stared at the ceiling, her face devoid of all expression.

At last, a tight smile cracked her icy lips. Palms flat, she pushed against her desk to roll back her cushy chair. Standing with deliberation, Shirley thrust out her stiff hand in formal congratulations. "Well, well, Tammy Fadler, you really did pass. Let me be the first to welcome you to Century 21 Showcase."

Chapter 27

Century 21 Showcase, 1988
Festus, Missouri

Getting Real

"Wha I nee to do nex?"

Shirley paused. "Excuse me?"

"I reh-dee go to wor. You say me wha I nee to do nex?"

"Ah, yes, so I did." Shirley nodded and took a deep breath. "Go see Claudia. She'll get your paperwork to send in for your license. And we'll guide you through the training programs you'll need." She waived a dismissive hand as she reached for her telephone.

"Buh wha wor I do to-day?"

"Work? Today? Ah, yes. Well," she kept dialing, "the first thing you need to do is go home and write down the names of one hundred people you know. We'll show you what to do after that." Shirley started speaking into the phone.

Tammy bobbed her head, mouthing a silent goodbye.

At home, she thought about everyone she knew: fellow employees and customers at Golde's, all her old bosses, wait staff and patrons at The Saigon Restaurant, classmates and teachers at Jefferson College, classmates and teachers at her children's school, friends, neighbors, relatives.

She wrote down every name she could come up with. She didn't quite have a hundred, but the list was long enough, comprehensive enough, that it startled her as much as it impressed her.

And it seemed to impress Shirley, too, whose eyes widened when she read the pages.

"What you need to do next is draft a letter of introduction," she said. "Explain that you're now a real estate agent. Tell them you need their help. Ask if they know of anyone who's thinking about buying or selling a house. Then, when you're finished, give it to Claudia. She'll read the letter through and help you fine tune it."

She instructed Tammy in the importance of follow-up phone calls and hand-written thank you notes, stressing their importance for something as minute as an appointment and as valuable as a sale.

"And there will be a few other things you'll need to work on, too."

Tammy had already figured that out.

Her language skills, most of all, needed attention.

Naturally outgoing, she knew how to approach people, how to be friendly, how to communicate. Those tools she had honed since her first job at MAC-V. But talking on the telephone, a vital part of this business, required a new skill set. People seemed to find it more difficult to understand her over the phone than when she dealt with them face to face.

It's my accent, she chastised herself. *I'll have to work on it, remember to wrap my tongue around every* thr, *remember to enunciate, and stop dropping my word endings like the officers' wives taught me back at Fort Meade.*

Oh, but the words, those phrases, that verbiage. It appeared that the real estate business required a vocabulary unique to itself.

It's like learning another foreign language, and I haven't even mastered English yet!

The following days proved to Tammy that there were a million things she didn't know about the real estate business, too. And, it seemed, the business of real estate wasn't just about the clients.

In the office, she first noticed the calculating quips followed by small smiles. Next, there were snippy jokes accompanied by a short laugh or two.

She wasn't blind to the tension around her; she sensed the differences that set her apart from the other agents. She understood that those cutting comments were aimed at *her.* The jabbing jokes were about *her.*

About her brown, beat-up Datsun in the parking lot, about her simple clothes, and—why not?—about her struggling English.

It hurt. It made her second guess her decision to start a new career with few skills and little knowledge.

How can I get on the phone and make cold calls to people that I hardly know? They can't even understand me.

1. I don't speak the proper English.

2. I don't wear the expensive outfits.

3. I don't drive the fancy car.

And how will I ever be able to, to just come right out and ask people for their business? Let me *sell your home. Let* me *help you buy a house. Give your business to* me, *to foreign little*

Tammy Fadler. The little foreign lady who can't speak properly and whose clothes aren't professional and whose rusted-out Datsun is falling apart.

Please, give your business to me, Me, ME. *Why? Because . . .*

1. because I want the freedom and flexibility to spend time at home with Ginny and Richie.

2. because I need money to make a living, to pay my bills.

3. because I need money to send to Saigon.

4. because I need to establish a career so I can sponsor my family to America where they, too, can have a future.

That's why!

Although she had no answers for this unexplored frontier ahead of her, Tammy had no doubts about the reasons she had committed—was determined to stay committed—to this new career with its endless lists of names, letters of introduction, phone script steps and motivational points. She chanted her own list of reasons, her needs, her *motivations* again and again, a litany to remind and encourage herself, especially at office meetings, when she felt

a. inadequate,
b. ill-equipped and
c. unprepared.

One day, Tammy was confronted at work and instructed—politely but firmly—that she needed to dress professionally. At Century 21, that meant wearing their signature gold jacket with smart, dark dress slacks. She flinched. Not only must she shell out money she didn't have for clothes she couldn't afford, but she was being required to wear *gold*.

Not flattering red, not traditional Vietnamese white or black. Gold!

Gold was the color of dirty straw and moldy lemons. She hated the color gold. She looked awful in gold. It dulled her hair. It sallowed her skin. It jaundiced her eyes. Gold literally sucked the vitality from her. She couldn't, she simply could *not* wear that awful color.

Tammy bought the gold jacket. And the classic dress slacks. In *brown*, of all colors!

She had officially faced, and met, her first challenge.

✦ ✦ ✦

Shirley provided her eager new agent with a list:

Sound Business Practices:

1. Remember that you are an independent contractor, working for yourself.
2. Know how to talk to people.
3. Make cold calls.
4. Knock on doors.
5. Prospect "For Sale by Owner" properties.
6. Follow the Dialog Script.
7. Be able to qualify clients.
8. Keep filling the pipeline.
9. Set goals and work toward them.
10. Aim high.

Tammy didn't question Shirley's advice. She simply smiled and said, "You my boss!"

Neither did she balk or complain. Instead, she took Shirley at her word because, inherently, she recognized the practices as essential to building her business. She took each idea to heart.

Every morning, she looked at expired listings, properties that hadn't sold. She phoned or drove to each address. She left her business card in doors, practiced her dialog (and her English), made cold calls (the magical twenty that Shirley advised—and sometimes even beyond) and prospected clients. She did it all without reservation or hesitation.

Especially the goals.

Ever practical, Tammy laid out the figures for her household budget. She knew exactly how much she needed to provide for her family of three. Maybe even give her children the little luxuries never possible during her own childhood. She set her first goal: Make $12,000 in one year.

Broken down, that translated to a monthly earning of more than $1,000. Could she really do it? The average house was selling for $45,000. With her commission split, she'd need to sell, let's see now, how many houses?

She swallowed back her uncertainty and underlined her goal.

$12,000 in the next year

Her first listing happened so quickly that it stunned everyone at the office.

Following the work practices Shirley detailed for her, Tammy placed a follow-up call to Kenny, a Festus businessman and longtime customer at her restaurant.

"Did you get my ler-rur, Ken-nee?"

"Yeah, I got it," he said. "By the way, I sure miss those midnight breakfasts at The Saigon, Tammy."

"Me, too."

"So what's this about you switching jobs, kiddo? Jumping the boat, are you? What's up with that?"

She followed the phone script she had worked through at the office. "I wan to give new cur-eer a chanz. Do you have nee for Ree-a-stay, Ken-nee?"

"No, honey, I don't."

"You know in-nee one who do?"

"No, sorry, I . . . hey, wait a sec. Yeah, maybe I do know someone, Tammy! Mrs. Laburay just down the street from me. I believe they're fixing up that rental house, getting it ready to sell sometime soon."

Tammy couldn't keep the excitement from her voice. "You tink dey mine I phone dem?"

"No, I'm pretty sure they wouldn't mind."

She read the next point on her script. "It okay I tell you say me?"

"Sure, honey."

"Tanx, Ken-nee. You goo frien!"

Tammy wasted no time contacting Mrs. Laburay—after she'd conscientiously penned a hand-written note of appreciation to Kenny for his referral.

"Ken-nee say me abou dis," she explained to her prospective client, still following the script. "Are you hav-een a Ree-a-tur? Can I tawk you abou dis?"

"Certainly," agreed the woman, with no hesitation in her voice.

She had landed a client, her first client! The rental, listed at $65,000, sold before the month, her first month at Century 21 Showcase, was over.

It was official. Tammy had successfully completed the sale of a house. Her very first sale!

And then the unimaginable happened: Even before closing on the Laburay house, Tammy sold a second investment property, proving to herself that she'd chosen the right career, after all.

✦ ✦ ✦

When Shirley suggested she attend a workshop sponsored by Century 21, Tammy snapped up the opportunity. Floyd Wickman's National Sweathogs Training Program encouraged realtors to make the goals of clients and customers a top priority and espoused the Game of Numbers to jump-start a career: The more phone calls you make, the more appointments you get; the more appointments you get, the more business you generate. To succeed in this business, they repeated again and again, you must, you must, you *must* keep calling until you get an appointment.

It all made sense, good sense, to Tammy. Besides, a competition ensued.

Sweathogs distributed a specific dialog script to practice for cold calls. Agents were instructed to track their calls and the activity those calls generated and report each week. Their statistics proved that, on average, agents would need to contact three people to get one appointment and they would need three appointments to produce one transaction. Sweathogs would log the numbers at each workshop to decide the final winner.

And Tammy was determined to be that winner.

One day, she phoned more than a hundred people without booking a single appointment.

"Call again," a few said.

"Maybe later," some promised.

"Contact me sometime in the future," others brushed her off.

She called fifty-eight more with the same results. *What happened to three phone calls, one appointment?* she grouched. *So much for their Game of Numbers.*

Still, she persisted. She would not show up at Sweathogs that week without reaching her quota of three. After all, wasn't that what a challenge was all about? Tammy pulled the telephone in front of her and started dialing. By the end of the Sweathogs Program, she had reached her goal. Not only had she accumulated the most units, but she led in volume and money. She earned Top Lister and Top Overall Producer.

Sweathogs, it turned out, was merely her practice field. Just as she'd been promised, her consistency grew a clientele (rather than seeming bothered by her English, she noticed, they paid attention when she spoke) and her sales transactions grew incrementally. By the end of her first full year with Century 21, Tammy was recognized—by both her local agency and by the region—as a "Multi-Million Dollar Producer."

Even better, she earned $17,000 that first year, a full $5,000 more than she'd hoped. She'd made money to provide for Ginny and Richie with enough left to set aside for her family's sponsorship. Hard work in real estate, she decided, ensured good fortune.

Tammy had accomplished the last item on the list of Shirley's business practices. She had set her goals; she had worked toward them, and she had aimed high.

She was, indeed, the winner!

CHAPTER 28

Century 21 Showcase, 1991
Festus, Missouri

Making Change

Already late for her appointment, Tammy paused at the front desk.

"Can you tek top led-dur to mail, pleez?"

While her left arm wrestled with her coat and purse, she tried to loosen the envelope without dropping the stack of the paperwork clenched in her right hand. "Here, Dora, it nee a stam."

The receptionist reached for it. "Certainly, Tammy, one stamp. That will be twenty-nine cents."

Tammy gritted her teeth to control her temper. "I pay lay-rur. I got to go."

"But, you know the rules."

Oh, she knew the rules all right and she had no time to argue about them right now with a client twiddling his thumbs on Main Street. Besides, there had been a listing-price change for the Wilson property, meaning it was imperative that this form go out in today's mail.

"Puh it on my tab!" Tammy tossed the sarcastic words over her shoulder as she tore out the door.

Tammy seethed all the way to her appointment, disgruntled at the recent petty procedures that had filtered down from Century 21 to its franchises.

Charging the brokers for office supplies! A nickel for each sheet of letterhead, a dime for an envelope. And postage! She took a deep breath to release the tension in her jaw.

Tammy had grown increasingly unhappy at the agency of late.

With a fistful of flattering awards and a wall full of plaques, she'd been dubbed a "rising star" in the industry. In 1989 she was honored as Multi-Million Dollar Producer, in 1990 Top Listing Agent, Top Selling Agent and Top Agent in a four-state region. She was the company's Golden Girl, the platform example.

"Keep your eye on that little Tammy Fadler. If she can make it in this business, you can, too!" speakers proclaimed.

Now more than ever, headquarters pushed brokers harder to earn more money while *they* tightened their office purse strings, making life difficult for a top agent like Tammy. The permeating attitude implied that an agency was better off having ten agents at the $1 million level than one agent producing $10 million. If a $10 million producer walked out the door, they reasoned, all that profit would go with them.

Headquarters maintained that there was "no room for a *prima donna* in an office." They said that a *prima donna* was a sore thumb that demanded attention and more services than a regular agent. They said it was clearly a mistake to cater to those high producers.

Well, I say *you're making it difficult for a top agent like me. I can't believe you're treating your number-one producer this way.*

Tammy's workload had grown at the same rate as her clientele increased. Busy beyond belief, she had no assistant, no staff, no one to attend to the small details, the sales listings, the follow-ups, the letters, the ever-cumbersome paper trail. Fatigue was her constant companion.

And now, as if that weren't bad enough, they wanted her to keep change on hand for each stamp she used.

A stamp! Well, she heaved a sigh of disgust, *that's the frond that bowed the water buffalo's back!*

A part of her remained loyal, grateful, to Century 21 and always would. Once Tammy proved her sincerity and work ethic, Shirley had tucked Tammy under her wing, teaching and mentoring. She also pushed and challenged.

"A Dale Carnegie course is being offered in Festus," Shirley had said during the early months of Tammy's initiation into real estate. "Would you consider attending?"

"Shure." Tammy had no clue what a Dale Carnegie was, but she always latched onto Shirley's suggestions.

"It will be a great chance for you to improve your communication skills," Shirley pointed out.

It was no secret that Tammy struggled with her presentations and wasn't always able to express her thoughts in a way her clients could understand, causing a level of frustration on both sides of the desk. She often wished for more confidence, a weakness she despised in herself. In her ongoing journey toward personal growth in order to better serve her customers, she was willing to do anything. Anything. Even expose her failings in order to tackle the unknown. In this case, a Carnegie course.

"The tuition is twelve hundred dollars. Now, now," Shirley held up a palm at Tammy's gasp. "I know that's a lot for you to come up with so quickly." She deliberated. "I could advance you the money. Would that be agreeable?"

Tammy nodded.

"At each of your next twelve closings, we could hold back one hundred dollars. What do you think? Does that sound doable to you?"

"I woo love to do thah! Ih woo hel me so much!" She had beamed, delighted to let Shirley smooth her path to self improvement.

Frowning at her tardiness—Tammy prided herself on meeting with clients punctually—she nosed her car into the first parking spot she found near Main Street. She owed a lot to this agency. She knew that. But the current situation of office penny-pinching made her twitch with impatience.

Which was probably why she was so open to a new opportunity when a realtor friend approached her a few days later.

"What are you up to now?" asked Rhonda.

"You not bee-lee what hap-pin-neen at my of-fiss!" Tammy shared her complaints.

Rhonda rolled her eyes. "Boy, do I understand! I left Century 21 over a three dollar advertising bill." She leaned closer. "There's something going on, Tammy, something you should be part of."

Tammy cocked her head. "Oh?"

"Uh huh. A few of us are going to meet and discuss an idea I have. Sunny invited us to his house. You've got to come!"

Rhonda gave her directions, promising, "It will be worth your time, just you wait and see."

Tammy felt the tension as soon as she walked into the room late that night. "Hi, Sun-nee. Hel-lo Rhonda . . ." Her voice trailed off when she noticed Mimi, a highly successful agent with a competing agency and Tammy's secret idol. "Wha go on here?"

Sunny handed her a mug of coffee. "Well, Tammy, we have a proposition and we'd like to get your input."

"Yes?" Tammy blew away a tendril of steam, waiting for her drink to cool. "Wha on yur mine?"

"Sit down, and we'll tell you."

Rhonda and Mimi detailed their dissatisfaction with their agencies. They were disgruntled with policy, unhappy with practices and displeased at payout. And they knew that Tammy, too, had similar complaints with the methods of traditional offices.

"We're all tired of getting knocked down!"

They had an idea they wanted to share. An idea especially attractive to top agents like themselves. They wanted to bring RE/MAX to Jefferson County

RE/MAX, with its 100% Commission Concept.

Not the traditional split. The full commission.

Engrossed in their fervor, Tammy set her coffee on the table. This was no time for distractions. "How ih can hap-pin?"

And that's when they fleshed out a daring plan.

"We're thinking about starting up our own agency, an agency based on this concept. And we'd like you to join us."

"Fran-chize?"

Mimi nodded. "Absolutely. A RE/MAX franchise."

"Just think, Tammy, we'd be working for ourselves!" Rhonda's eyes glowed. "*We* would be the decision makers. *We* would determine office policy."

"How ih wor?"

Her friends explained exactly how it worked, laying out their thought process for her to examine. Sunny, with his analytical mind and legal expertise, agreed to broker the office, allowing the women to continue fulfilling their roles as top producers. The four of them would make this company an overnight success.

Tammy liked what they'd come up with. Although the idea of committing to a monthly fee of $2,000–$2,400 for the privilege of being in an office daunted her.

Wouldn't that put the agent at risk each month? She couldn't help wondering if she had what it took to succeed under a plan like this.

Rhonda laid out the figures with solemn reassurances that they would make certain Tammy generated the sales she needed to stay in the black. "You can do this, Tammy. We know you can."

Tammy was beginning to think so, too. *If* they could finance the business.

"How much mon-nee?" Tammy asked.

Her mind toyed with the numbers Rhonda tossed out. About $100,000 to get the new agency up and running, office setup, phones, signage; another $25,000 for the franchise. Even with a four-way split between them, that would make her share . . . Tammy's eyes widened at the amount.

"But don't let that scare you."

Oh, but it did. Letters had been flying back and forth from Vietnam lately, and she was inching toward her dream of relocating her family to America. However, it took a lot of money to accomplish—airfare for each person, fees to the Vietnamese government, cash for under-the-table bribes to corrupt Communist officials. Some of the paperwork was already in the pipeline for Ma, Ba and the five youngest children. Even so, her goal had spread its arms to embrace her older siblings, their spouses and the children they were producing.

Tammy rubbed damp palms against her black dress pants.

Even with the three of them, all top agents with proven track records, the dollars daunted her. Her goal of a united family directed every decision in her life. She simply couldn't put her dream at risk.

Sunny understood her reluctance. "How about I buy the franchise and be the broker?" He rubbed the stubble on his chin, deep in thought. "I can take out a mortgage on my house if you will commit to pay your share."

"We nee one mohr," she said. "We nee one mohr to share beez-nuss coss."

"Another agent to cover office expenses would give everyone a boost of confidence," Sunny said.

"What about Sherry?" Rhonda offered. "That little Southern gal has a lot on the ball. She would be a dynamic addition to our team."

They all agreed. Sherry, too, was a top producer. Disregarding the late hour, Sunny picked up the telephone and dialed.

"What do you mean, she's ready for bed? Tell Sherry to grab her robe and get on over here. What? Then you drive her, Mickey. You're her husband; make her come. This is important. Anyway, we might need you to help us talk her into something."

Sherry's husband Mickey did help them convince her. With her on board, they numbered five. The secretive meeting stretched into the dark hours of night as the powerful group of real estate agents fine-tuned their plan.

At last, Rhonda yawned. "Well, folks, I'm tired. I was out late last night and really need to get some sleep."

They decided it was time to call it quits.

Each one of them had firmly pledged their full support. Mimi Cook. Rhonda Kister. Sherry Fincher. Sunny Vincent. Tammy Fadler. All leading producers in their respective agencies. Leaders now making leadership decisions.

Tammy's heart fluttered.

Excitement? No doubt.

Fear? Of course.

But it was guilt—guilt, plain and simple—that pricked her conscience and made her pulse race.

In spite of her frustrations with Century 21, Tammy's loyalty to Shirley burned deep. Could she really do this? Could she leave her mentor, her benefactor, her teacher? Shirley had believed in Tammy, encouraged her and even pushed her. And now, now Tammy was quitting? Walking away from the person who had helped her reach this level of production and financial security?

The new partners said their goodbyes and headed out the door for their cars and homes.

"We can make this happen," someone whispered through the dark. "We can really do this!"

They made a pact to keep the idea to themselves until everything was set to go. A lot of pins would tumble when the five of them turned in their resignations at the agencies where they felt mistreated.

Elephants won't bite, thought Tammy, *but mosquitoes do.*

Chapter 29

Howard Brinton Star Power, 1994
Aspen, Colorado

Reaping the Rewards

"This requires a change of mindset, people." The speaker rose on the balls of his feet as he leaned across the podium to emphasize his point. "And this complete change of mindset will alter your methods of production and generate more sales. Believe me, it will increase your monthly volume."

A shiver started in Tammy's stomach and spread until she was nearly twitching in her eagerness to apply the principles she was learning. She believed, all right. She could hardly wait to fly back to Festus, roll up her sleeves and get started.

Well, except for the part of her that wanted to stay. This was, after all, the first real luxury vacation she'd had since she came to America in 1973. In great part, that was the reason she'd scraped up the money to come.

"You'll love 'Colorful Colorado,'" friends had enthused when she waved the brochure beneath their noses, mentioning her temptation to attend the seminar. "And Aspen is right in the heart of the Rockies, surrounded by some of the most spectacular scenery in the whole country!"

They were right, she decided, as she glanced out the window of the hotel to take in the breathtaking view of Ponderosa pines and hazy mountain ranges.

She pulled her gaze back to the speaker, trying to focus on his closing remarks.

"Remember, don't look at real estate as simply a way to make a living. Treat it like a bona fide business." The gold watch at his wrist winked in a shaft of sunlight. "Those of us here at Star Power have given you the strategies, tools and secrets to raise your standard of service and take your business to the next level. We want you to break the glass ceiling. Find the courage to risk, the faith to believe and the will to succeed!"

Standing with the others to applaud the gentleman, Tammy found her self caught up in the inspirational lyrics of the closing music, "Nothing's going to stop us now." Her mind toyed with his final words: *Break the glass ceiling with the courage to risk, the faith to believe and the will to succeed.*

She could relate to that challenge. She had dared to do so many things, all to achieve her dream of a better life for herself and her family. Already, it was paying off. Ginny and Richie were dedicated high school students. Tammy had instilled in them the same respect she had had for teachers and learning. Oh, she had the will to succeed, all right. Some called her bullheaded; she saw herself as goal oriented. And, now, her chief goal centered on those she'd left behind in Khanh Hoi.

Her thoughts raced in several directions, trying to integrate the messages she had heard with her actual work philosophy at RE/MAX, the means to her end goal.

Well, why not? Why not go back to Festus with a new goal? Why not figure out a way to take the things she'd learned here and shift her business to a new level, like the speaker urged?

She was already the renegade agent in the office, the only one who'd pushed the status quo by hiring her own staff as her workload grew. Not everyone approved. Some of the agents were miffed that her larger presence at RE/MAX tied up the phone lines and ate away at office resources, even though she had increased her monthly share of the business expenses they split among them.

She'd hired Tracey Smart as her full-time personal assistant. Next, she added buying agents Rick Ramsey and Brenda Williamson. And, when Dick approached her about a job in real estate after he left Motorola, she brought him in as a buying agent, too. A few people raised their brows, but she shrugged off their speculation and doubts. Dick was still the father of her children. He was a good man. He was, after all, family.

Break the glass ceiling with the courage to risk, the faith to believe and the will to succeed.

Her sixteen-hour work days at the agency sapped Tammy's energy just as surely as had the pails of water she toted to the swine in Khanh Hoi. Stress had a choke hold on her life. Responsibilities crowded her calendar. Close to burnout from the load she carried, she immediately recognized the "glass ceiling" concept bandied about these past few days.

Not only did she understand it, she had lived it. Lived it, and hoped to smash it into tiny shards.

Tammy wanted to do more than get by. She'd spent her entire life getting by. She wanted to make money. Real money. Money enough to sponsor the ever-growing list of brothers-in-law, sisters-in-law, nieces and nephews anxious to leave Vietnam. The concepts espoused at Star Power supported her in that goal.

But, did she have what it would take to change her ways and push her career in a new direction? To continue bucking the system at RE/MAX?

When the five of them had originally joined the franchise, they'd left a few shipwrecks in their wake. Some of the flotsam that floated to shore had not been salvageable. Relationships were tarnished and feelings bruised. Forced to leave behind her listings at Century 21, she'd come to RE/MAX wearing nothing but a barrel to start over again.

Yet, here she was, three years later, armed with her pioneering spirit and eager to rock the boat once more.

Even discounting their obvious charisma and wit in their coaching styles, Tammy was impressed and inspired by the cast of champions who presented at Star Power. Their passion re-ignited hers when they urged, "Be self-starters. Energize your business. Enthuse your clients. Elevate your success."

Could she?

Dare she accept the challenge to change?

Before the crowd could leave, energetic Tony DiCello grabbed the microphone. "Those of you who want to change your life, meet back here this afternoon for a special program to learn about Dr. Fred Grosse. I guarantee you won't regret it!"

Change? Did he say change?

Tammy returned promptly at 5:30 p.m. She listened closely to the presentation by Tony, Tim Baker and Bob Wolf, all leading agents in the industry. She leaned forward when they bragged about the coaching prowess of Dr. Fred Grosse and the powerful potential for change it would infuse in their lives.

"Are you interested in starting a group to work with Dr. Fred?" asked Tony from the platform. "We need you to commit. Go home, think it over and show your commitment by sending a check. If enough people do this, we'll start a group."

Tammy left the seminar refreshed, fired up. She pondered all she'd heard, returning to RE/MAX with a vision, a vision of her future. It was a vision she was certain she could fulfill if she could harness the guidance of this coach who would inspire her to stretch. That's what she wanted, to stretch as far as she could go.

The courage to risk, the faith to believe and the will to succeed.

Without a second thought, she sent in the requested $750 check, payable to Tony DiCello.

✦ ✦ ✦

During the next few years, Tammy continued to invest in herself. She attended seminars by Les Brown and Zig Ziglar and other motivational speakers, traveled to work under Dr. Fred and counted each plane trip as a vacation. A working vacation. From the East Coast to the West Coast to Cancun and farther, she followed her dream and honed her skills, making new contacts and forming lasting friendships.

Her Tuesday Sisters were a natural outgrowth of these shared experiences. Gail French, Glenda Williamson and Pat Sherman were like-minded women she'd met on her quest to self improvement, realtors whose aims and personalities meshed with her own. The four of them registered for the same events, shared rooms and traveled together. To extend their pleasure in each other's company, they began a weekly conference call, devoting Tuesday mornings to mentor and support each other.

The Tuesday Sisters held each other accountable to goals while taking ample time to share successes and moan disappointments. They laughed and they cried and they found ways to meet and to play.

Tammy didn't just listen to the messages of the industry gurus; she heard them. Heard them and took them to heart.

"Get by giving."

"Perspire to aspire."

"Become the person you want to be."

As a result, her sales volume soared and garnered a lot of attention locally and beyond. She was recognized as #1 Realtor in Jefferson County, listed in the "Best of the Best Poll" by the *Jefferson County Suburban Journal*. The *St. Louis Business Journal* dubbed her Highest Selling Agent in the St. Louis Metropolitan Area. She was named Best in Client Satisfaction Real Estate Agent by *St. Louis Magazine*. She was inducted into RE/MAX's President's and Platinum clubs.

The awards came so fast, she lost track or didn't keep track. Perhaps because, in her eyes, the most important compensation and recognition for her efforts wasn't a plaque, a certificate or a trophy.

The prize she coveted was, quite simply, family.

✦ ✦ ✦

In February of 1993, Tammy had finally gotten some of her family out of Saigon. She gathered them into her arms at the St. Louis Airport, nestling them against the pounding in her breast exactly two decades—a lengthy, full twenty years—since she'd last seen them.

Those years had not been kind. She saw how war and worry had creased Ma's aging face. She noticed how drudgery and deprivation had hunched dear Ba's thin frame. Yet pure joy and relief scattered a confetti of glistening tears over their reunion, softening the agony of lost years in the hopeful promise of a comfortable future.

What a joy it was to introduce Ginny and Richie to Ba and Ma. But Tammy hardly recognized the crowd who came with them. She sorted through them like bright coins, making certain each was accounted for. Brother Ten, Brother Eleven, Brother Twelve—no longer the rambunctious boys she remembered, but handsome men, all still single. Pretty Sister Thirteen, who'd been a newborn when Tammy left Saigon, now twenty years old. Smiling Brother Eight and Brother Seven.

No, no, not Brother Seven, the one among them who'd been brainwashed by the Communists and refused to accompany the others to America. Even though she'd labored over his paperwork, paid the bribes and made the arrangements. She stiffened, refusing to let any member of her family be counted as a loss, a casualty of their circumstances. She would try again until Brother Seven came.

Surely, he would come.

"What, Ma?" Tammy bent lower, hugging her mother close to hear her murmurings above the excited chatter.

"How?" asked Ma, her dazed eyes skittering over a bevy of noisy travelers in the airport who were making phone calls, consulting their wrist watches and greeting loved ones.

"How? How what, Ma?"

"How do you know them apart, Daughter Two? They all look alike, these Americans. See?" She pointed around the terminal. "They all dress alike. They all talk funny. How do you know them apart?"

Tammy grinned.

Then she giggled.

When Ma frowned, Tammy could no longer contain herself. Her giggles erupted into a hearty bellow. She laughed and laughed until her laughter turned into hiccups. Which made her laugh again.

Wiping the moisture from her eyes, she pulled Ma into another tight embrace. For the pure joy of it. And because, well, because now she could and would be able to again and again in the years stretching before them.

Over the top of Ma's head, Tammy inspected the others, recognizing the dazed looks in their eyes, remembering her own fatigue after the grueling trip to America. She squeezed her mother one last time and pulled away when Ma grunted.

"Come, everyone," Tammy motioned. "Let's get you home. We can visit tomorrow when you're all rested."

Tomorrow, she thought, liking the sound of it. *We'll have time together then and ever after.*

Tomorrow.

The word held a wealth of promise.

CHAPTER 30

Signature Properties, 2000
Festus, Missouri

Flying Solo

Tension in the RE/MAX office was palpable.

Tammy's pioneering spirit had blazed a trail for the buyer agents she'd hired and their combined success set a stellar production level in her corner of the building. Her determination to touch untouched territory with her controversial concepts increased the friction between her and some of the other agents until, one day, she took a deep breath and plunged into the murky waters of the unknown.

Tammy set up her own business: Tammy Fadler Real Estate.

Her decision was fraught with fear. As the sole owner of an independent agency, she would have no franchise behind her.

There would be no RE/MAX, no Century 21, no big name affiliation at all.

Without someone backing her, there would be neither security nor recognition. Would anyone bother to do business with her?

"Create your own brand," was the advice she'd heard at Star Power. Tupper Briggs, the agent of a successful, independent agency in Evergreen, Colorado, insisted it was the key to his success—Talk to Tupper, Excellence in Real Estate.

A brand, she thought, *I just need to come up with an appealing brand. Something that reflects me.*

She remembered Ba's farewell so many years ago: "Remember, *con*, your name is your only possession of real value. See that you honor it."

After giving it some consideration, she arrived at a slogan of her own: Talk to Tammy.

Undaunted at the possibility of rejection, she was never reluctant to phone a prospect or communicate with a client. Tammy was always ready to talk! However, the irony of the phrase was not lost on her. As someone who still spoke with a distinctive accent, she'd worked hard to overcome her initial insecurities.

Tammy purchased two buildings in downtown Festus on Main Street. She rented out the larger one and moved her staff into the smaller one next door before hanging out her sign, ready for business.

And she got it.

She and her employees achieved listing after listing, sale after sale. Tammy Fadler Real Estate was definitely a player to be reckoned with in the realty game. Tammy's self discipline, her drive and her just-do-it philosophy paid off. In the process of elevating her success, she made an important discovery:

People hadn't done business with a big company logo; they had always done business with her.

Her.

Not RE/MAX, not Century 21, but her.

Clients sought out little Tammy Fadler—with her fifth-grade education, $10 in her pocket and a one-way ticket to the wrong city in America.

Customers came because they liked her and respected her work ethic. They knew she'd get the job done. And, of course, she did. They gave her repeat business because of her level of service. In return, they made referrals, generating yet more business.

Transactions multiplied and monthly volume gained momentum.

Tammy moved into the larger building next door. She rented out the smaller one to an attorney. She changed her company's name to the more formal Signature Properties.

And she attended additional Star Power events, impressed by magnetic motivational speakers who addressed profitability through the use of team building and life balance to profoundly improve the quality of both the realtors' businesses and their personal lives.

"Work isn't life. Work supports life," she heard again and again.

Enthralled with the novel concept, Tammy gained new insight. For the first time ever, she thought about the impact of work on her personal priorities and important relationships and resolved to initiate life changes. She didn't just want to be a person who *made* a million dollars, she concluded, she wanted to *become* a million-dollar person.

With that ideal before her, Tammy developed a destiny statement for herself, promising:

To live my life to the fullest, to walk my talk and to be in the present with every breath I take.

Encouraged by the lessons she was learning from the platform, she returned from another seminar armed with a mission statement she had developed for Signature Properties:

To provide first-class service with honesty, integrity, promptness and an "It's my pleasure" attitude to every client we serve. To have a balanced life while maintaining the market share and giving back to our community. Anything less than excellence is unacceptable.

All these changes affected her productivity which, in turn, drew attention. *The Residential Specialist* magazine highlighted her in "Top Producer Profiles." She participated in the "Real Estate LIVE! Training Video." *Jefferson County Business Journal* interviewed her for their "Movers and Shakers" issue in December of 2005 as did *REALTOR Magazine* that same year.

Tammy hired more agents, building her team to ten, and taught them her business philosophy—parts of which, she learned to her amusement, harkened back to the open-air marketplace of her youth in Khanh Hoi. Stylized pearls of wisdom that defined her personal business practices:

1. Form smart partnerships. (Thuan had something Phuong wanted; Phuong had something Thuan wanted.)

2. Qualify your prospects. (A live fish is always worth more than a dead fish.)
3. Keep calling until you get a "yes." (There are fish to sell before we eat.)
4. Budget your time; budget your resources. (Make enough profit to pay for today's stall and tomorrow's supply of fish.)
5. Exceed your customers' expectations. (It was a daily fight for survival and the marketplace was her battleground.)
6. Ask for the sale. (Buy *my* fish.)

Setting her sights still higher, Tammy added a sister company, Commercial International Properties, in 2006. The growing list of professional designations behind her name was an alphabet soup that included CRS, GRI and ABR. She earned her DTM from Toastmasters International and became a Howard Brinton Star Power Speaker, internalizing the Howard Brinton philosophy: Use an "It's my pleasure" approach accompanied by a "Ritz-Carlton-type service." She attended CEO Summits and joined a CEO Mastermind Group.

In her eyes, it all simply represented more opportunities to learn, a continuing education and additional stepping stones on her pathway to personal growth.

Yet, along the way, she never lost track of family.

After the first group of seven arrived in 1993, Tammy pumped a new batch of paperwork through the sponsorship pipeline. Then, it seemed, her family came like hungry shoppers drawn to the vendor's stall.

In February of 1998, she greeted Sister Five, her husband and two children. Brother Six, his wife and two children. Sister Nine, her husband and two children. Twelve in all, who crowded temporarily into Ma and Ba's house until Tammy could get them settled in places of their own. Brother Four joined them in July of that year. In 1999, widowed Sister Three landed in St. Louis with her son and daughter. Brother Four's wife came soon after.

Gradually, Tammy felt their individual lives entwine with hers like elaborate stitches embroidering an empty canvas.

Watching her two-year-old nephew play in his new yard brought Tammy comfort.

No stray bullets in this neighborhood, she congratulated herself.

Watching her sixteen-year-old niece blossom brought her joy.

No soldier will ever haul her from her bed and steal her away, she assured herself.

Watching Ma and Ba surrounded by healthy, carefree grandchildren brought her a full measure of satisfaction.

None of them will ever live in fear again, she vowed.

Her family members could do and become whatever they wanted in the Land of Opportunity.

Yet, even in the midst of so much joy, one loose thread threatened to unravel her dream. Tammy had filed paperwork a second time for Brother Seven and made all the arrangements to satisfy governments on both continents. She'd sent letters and paid bribes. Once again, he balked, changed his mind, refused to come, holding his firm allegiance to the Communist government.

Tammy tightened her mouth in frustration.

Haven't I sacrificed enough? I can't give up another loved one.

She closed her eyes, remembering an earlier loss: Khai, the man she'd left behind.

Khai had promised he would find her again one day. And he finally had. From his younger sister, who remained a friend of Tammy's Sister Five, he'd gotten her parents' telephone number. They had all happened to be present one Sunday when he called.

"He wants to talk with you." Sister Five handed the receiver to Tammy, who waved her open palms in frantic refusal.

"No!" she whispered. "Tell him I'm not here."

"But he asks for you."

"No!" she repeated, her refusal adamant. "You've got to tell him I'm not here."

Tammy watched her sister fumble with the receiver, her face etched with uncertainty.

Tammy had received a letter from Sister Five some years earlier with the information that Khai survived the war. Sister Five wrote about an invitation she accepted to accompany his family to the re-education camp where he had been taken.

Respectfully, she stood back while he greeted his parents, but when he saw her, Khai ran to embrace the young woman who looked so much like Thuận. Startled at his ardor, Sister Five extracted herself from his arms.

"Obviously," she'd written, "Khai still holds strong feelings for you."

And now he was on the phone.

From Sister Five, Tammy already knew that Khai later married in Vietnam and, some time after, immigrated with his wife and children to America.

Texas, she had mused. *Not so far from St. Louis. Maybe an easy two-hour flight?* The mere thought made her tingle.

Deep in her heart, Tammy knew if she spoke with Khai, heard the familiar timbre of his voice, she would be tempted to see him. She knew she needed to temper her young-girl yearnings with a wiser woman's prudence. She also knew she couldn't live with herself if her actions, her presence, broke apart his family.

No, no. I made the right decision, she assured herself once again, from the vantage point of time and distance. *Khai had already built a new life—and so had I. It was better that we travel our own paths. It was the honorable solution.*

Even so, the loss still nagged at her, years later, questioning her choice. Whispering an abiding uncertainty.

"What if . . . what if . . . what . . . if?"

CHAPTER 31

In air and on land, 2001
From the United States of America
to Sài Gòn, Việt Nam

Going Back

She couldn't pull her gaze away from the vivid greens beneath the wide wings of the airplane.

Vibrant and verdant.

Alive.

This sweep of lush jungle was not the scarred, barren Việt Nam that haunted her dreams—the raging animal that snorted and bellowed through war's thunder, groaning from the pain of its searing wounds and unable to disguise its grotesque scars.

Afraid the surprisingly vivid view would disappear if she blinked, Tammy turned in her seat and pressed her nose against the cold glass of the window. There it was, winding through deltas, sweeping from North to South, the undeniable link in a country still struggling for unity: the long dragon tail of the Mekong River. The river that would lead her home.

Her heart pounded.

A part of Tammy always knew she would return to Việt Nam. Like unfinished business, the need to come back had dogged her waking thoughts for nearly three decades, until the burden of persistence was too heavy to carry any longer. She recognized that she must visit the country of her birth.

She needed to go back in order to move forward.

During the past several years, Tammy had experienced personal growth and healing from the deep "soul work" offered at conferences with Dr. Fred Grosse. So she jumped at the chance to attend the Fred 100 in Bali, a relatively short flight from the home of her memories. A couple of her Tuesday Sisters, Glenda and Gail (along with Gail's husband Nick, their Token Male and an honorary brother to them all), asked if they could accompany her when she made her pilgrimage back.

"Shure!" Tammy had quickly agreed. "It eezy. We tray the Hong Kong lay-over for Vietnam."

The trade, she knew, would benefit them all. She would be their personal tour guide; in return, they would lend their moral support for this journey to and through her past.

Suddenly, Tammy felt her palms sweat. She could no longer look out the window. Instead, she let Glenda distract her with idle comments about the conference.

". . . great opportunity to recharge, refocus and rejuvenate . . ."

Tammy didn't answer.

". . . see the countryside in Bali . . ."

Tammy felt an eerie, expectant calmness fall over her.

"We're approaching Tân Sơn Nhứt Airport," announced the captain from the cockpit. "Prepare for landing."

Tammy fumbled with her seatbelt. To her left, Glenda clicked her own before reaching across to help Tammy with hers. The jet banked, rolled and leveled. Tammy's stomach did the same.

And the young Thuận unexpectedly came to life.

Her eyes welled as a monsoon of memories rained down. Harsh, heart-breaking sobs erupted. They both startled and embarrassed her. When Glenda put an arm around Tammy's shoulder, Tammy allowed herself a short release of tears, but quickly struggled for a measure of control.

She focused out the window, straining for a glimpse of the old American airbase she remembered, where war planes once stood in rows like soldiers at attention. She pointed at towers and buildings, remnants of another era. Hand-me-downs from the U.S. government.

"See? Thah MAC-V, where I use work."

She leaned across the aisle for glimpses through the other window.

"An thah feeld? See thah feeld? Thah where . . . thah where . . . a yung boy . . ." Tammy choked back tears and clamped her lips tight.

The plane landed in the sunny haze of a tangerine-tinted day.

"Oh . . . my . . . God. I heer!"

The changes in the airport were pointedly noticeable. Tammy tensed when she recognized the enemy uniform of the Customs official. North Vietnamese. She set her teeth in an unnatural bite and tried to damper the cold flush of hatred that iced her veins.

And then she saw them at the end of the jetway, waiting in the crowd just beyond the fence.

Her family: An uncle. A sister-in-law. Brother Seven holding up a sign that spelled out her name.

Like shedding skin, Tammy flung her arms wide. And it was Thuận who raced to meet them.

✦ ✦ ✦

Over the next few days, Tammy enjoyed her role as tour guide for Glenda, Gail and Nick. They saw monuments, graveyards and museums. The vestiges of war. She took them through the heart of dense traffic, a constant race of cyclos, bicycles and ever-present scooters—often six across—darting in and out, honking, jockeying for position. She taught them how to eat with chopsticks and what to order at quaint coffee shops, fine restaurants and one-woman street stalls. She showed them magnificent French architecture, the impressive Presidential Palace and the live chickens in the marketplace.

She took them on a coastal excursion to the pristine beaches of Nha Trang and pointed out the peasants who still threshed rice by hand along the shoulders of Highway 1.

At times, Tammy felt she was the tourist.

Although the span of years hadn't altered many aspects in her homeland, she discovered parts of Sài Gòn had transformed under the new regime from bedraggled street urchin to bejeweled harlot who traded her favors to the highest bidder. She'd even changed her name to Thành phố Hồ Chí Minh.

Hồ Chí Minh City.

Tammy marveled at the stunning new Renaissance Hotel where she and her friends stayed and felt her veins turn to ice when she witnessed the class bias which barred her uncle and Brother Seven from the lobby. She cringed at the sight of

Communist flags fluttering from the old U.S. barracks and mourned naval ships deserted in the muddy river like unwanted war orphans. Fine hairs on the back of her neck stood on end during the two hours each morning when loud speakers broadcast a spate of government propaganda throughout the city.

Her city.

Tammy decided she needed to go home. Back to Khánh Hội.

Managing to set aside his stubborn refusal to leave Việt Nam and the resulting uneasiness between them, Tammy allowed Brother Seven to arrange an entire afternoon for her. Grinning as she mounted his moped, she slipped her arms around his waist. She tossed her head and laughed in delight, reveling in the luxury of a cooling breeze that lifted the tendrils of her long hair while she listened to Brother Seven point out landmarks and tell her stories steeped in the recollections they shared.

As she wandered the familiar neighborhood to visit a few of Má's old friends and a smattering of relatives, Tammy's long-forgotten images stacked up like street apartments, one on top of the other: A gossipy grandmother who ran a tea stall . . . The woody scent of freshly steamed rice . . . A noodle vendor with his pointy goatee . . . The sweet smell of sandalwood incense . . . Pesky flies buzzing bruised fruit.

From the vantage point of time, she viewed the sensory tableau as an explosion of people, places and events that had shaped the young Thuận, the determined girl who had been torn between familial obligations and the dawning realization of her own rights.

Tammy picked her way through the marketplace. It hadn't changed much, she decided; it still reeked of fish. But everything seemed smaller than she remembered.

"How can a twelve-by-twelve-foot house be even tinier than I thought?" she asked Brother Seven.

He shrugged; he simply didn't share her frame of reference. Tammy couldn't stop herself from comparing the properties she sold around St. Louis to these humble village homes. A simple kerosene burner for cooking and a few pots hanging on the wall sufficed for a kitchen. A single box bed with a handful of steps leading to a sleeping platform substituted as bedrooms. A thin wall shielded a primitive toilet and cold shower, unknown indoor conveniences when Tammy was a girl.

A small living space, indeed, for any family, but especially for her family. All fourteen of them once lived like this, she realized.

"How did Má ever manage?" she asked aloud.

But she already knew the answer to that question. Now, seeing the humble lifestyle and poverty of her war-torn homeland through the lens of a visitor, she truly understood the past.

Dear Má had done the best she could with what she had. Even if it meant watching an eight-year-old daughter lug her weight in water to tend the neighbors' swine. Even if it meant relying on a ten-year-old to sell fish in the market. Even if it meant denying education to a fifth grader for the greater good of the entire family.

Má simply did what she had to do.

✦ ✦ ✦

On Sunday morning, the Tuesday Sisters and Nick met for a champagne brunch at the Renaissance. As they lingered at the table, Tammy wove lively tales about her early years in

Việt Nam. Her friends laughed at her antics on the military bases and shed tears over her stories of GIs who never made it home.

But it was the memory of a frightened teenage Thuận that painted the most poignant picture.

During the aftermath of the Tết Offensive, Tammy explained, American troops, tanks and armed personnel had continued to patrol the streets of Sài Gòn while NVA snipers, still embedded in the city, maintained their bloody carnage. Even so, after finishing her salad-making shift at MAC-V one night, Thuận headed outside to grab her bicycle for the ride home through treacherous streets.

She had felt the explosion before she heard it.

Mortars!

Warfare belched from the rear perimeter of the airbase. Terrorists had breached the barbed-wire barricade!

Frigid fingers of fear clutched her throat. Scared, confused at the sudden chaos, Thuận stumbled through the dark while people shouted and raced past.

"Run!" someone yelled as large guns spat their venom into MAC-V.

Thuận ran.

"Get down!" someone hissed as a mortar flew overhead.

Thuận flopped to her belly.

"Lie low!" she heard through a spray of machine guns.

Thuận crawled, weight on her forearms, like a fire ant scurrying back to its mound. She flattened herself to the ground behind a hump of dirt and pushed the side of her face hard into the soil, willing herself to melt into the safe arms of the earth.

The hammering attack raged on.

The veins in her temples throbbed. Thuận shivered in the hot night. She tried to swallow, but her throat was as dry as a dirt road. Then, beneath the bedlam, she heard a faint mewl. An animal? No, no. Cautiously, she raised her head an inch or more to listen with both ears. It sounded like a child!

A child?

Thuận inched her way across the field, crawling until she found him. A young boy. From his size, no older than ten. He moaned.

"Are you okay?" She edged nearer. "Where is your mama? Where is your family?"

She reached for him and touched wet clothes. She sniffed her fingers. Her nostrils flared at the metallic scent of blood.

"Where are you hurt?"

He whimpered.

Thuận squeezed his hand. "Stay close to me. You'll be fine, you'll see."

She looked wildly around for help. No one was in sight.

"You wait here. I'll bring someone back with me." Her stomach clenched. "I'll come right back. I promise."

"Hold me." His plea was faint. Weak. "Please . . . hold . . . me."

Trembling, Thuận scooted into place and tenderly cradled his small head against her chest, pressing her wobbly chin into the softness of his hair. The spark of gunfire still lit the big sky. Sporadic mortars fell around their tiny claim in the open field. Yet, oddly enough, she heard it.

His final breath.

It was as quiet as a whisper; it was as soft as a sigh.

✦ ✦ ✦

Tammy looked into the moist eyes of her dear friends—Glenda, Gail, Nick—friends who supported her, hand in hand, shoulder to shoulder, back to back. She was humbled, grateful for the blessings that enriched the life she had discovered so far away from Việt Nam. Yet, it had been necessary for her to travel full circle in order to truly comprehend how her past affected her present.

She'd poured out her memories and emptied her heart. Now, she wept.

Surrounded by people who loved her, she wept for the young Vietnamese girl who, a victim of war and circumstance, accepted death as inevitable. She wept for the young boy who died in her arms. She wept for childless mothers and motherless children and innocent young men and tender young women and teenage boys who fought old men's battles.

Tammy shuddered at the horrors of war and the exorbitant price it demanded. So much innocence lost. Her childhood, like a multitude of others, was tarnished by those painful events. She mourned her youth. And more.

She ached over the defeat of a downtrodden people and a national pride that was trampled. She flinched at the changes she witnessed in her country and shuddered at the hated flag now hoisted in victory.

So much blood shed. So many lives lost. Tammy folded her arms tight to her chest and sobbed.

But even as she grieved, she felt cleansed and . . . complete somehow. Although her life would always be tinged by tragic memories, she knew the wounds would scab and finally heal, until only faint scars remained. Like the lush growth covering the war-ravaged jungles of Việt Nam, her new life was vibrant and verdant. *Alive* with possibility and potential.

Fortune had, indeed, found her.

In that instant, Tammy Fadler vowed to invite the young Thuận—and the past she symbolized—to probe and forge the glowing future spread before her.

Words from Tammy

At the urging of my mentor, Tom Hill, I first approached Carol Rehme with the invitation to write a short, personal story so I could share it with others. Barely knee-deep into the interviewing process, she exclaimed, "Your life is more than a mere story. It's an entire book!"

Although the resulting manuscript is my personal journey, I invite you to take it with me. Along the way, you'll meet a few of my heroes: business coaches, life coaches and friends who provided leadership, guidance and support when I needed it most.

Finding the Pearl is more than memoir or biography. I believe it speaks universal truths; I believe it translates into each person's story—the revelation that everything we need as individuals is already inside us, regardless of the circumstances of our past, where we came from, how much material goods we had or what happened to us. What *is* important is how we pick up the pieces and how we start again. I believe if we just press forward, we'll find our destiny and discover we're only three feet from the gold.

That moment of decision—when we say "Yes!" to our dreams, we find powerful forces existing beyond ourselves and our consciousness. Magically, Opportunity opens doors. Our paradigm shifts, stretching our attitudes and opinions, and our minds never go back to their old, original forms.

During the interview process of this project, so much was revealed to me. I recognized that some imperfect moments had changed my entire course at those crucial times when I didn't know where I was going or what would happen when I got there. But faith always guided me. Faith gave me hope, even while my mother's voice inside my head urged, "Just do! Just do! Do what you have to do."

I was struck by an important discovery: I have been blessed beyond measure by the people and events that shaped my life.

This leaves me to disclose the reservation I had about sharing my journey. I know the Vietnam Conflict was unpopular. Decades later, many who were *there* still search for inner peace and resolution. This book is my offering to those souls seeking reason and purpose in their war-ravaged memories.

I have no answers. Yet, even in the darkest and ugliest corners of that era, be assured that there existed goodness, hope and generosity. And, always, there were dreams. I know; mine were my lifeline.

The nearly 60,000 U.S. soldiers listed on the Vietnam Veterans Memorial Wall and the other one million nameless who forfeited their lives did not die in vain. Their faces and their sacrifices are not forgotten. As a small token, I offer heartfelt gratitude to them and their families in appreciation for my personal freedom and the hope and future of my entire family.

Words from Carol

Although, as a journalist and ghost writer, I've had many opportunities throughout my writing career to interview people, never before have I plumbed the depths of someone's mind and memory to this degree. Remarkably, Tammy was an obliging victim, willing to open herself to self-reflection and eventual public scrutiny by freely sharing her thoughts, reactions and emotions. We quickly connected at our initial meeting, kindred spirits in quirky ways. And our budding relationship grew the trust necessary to nourish a broad project like this one.

Even though Tammy and I are women of the same age, we grew up on opposite sides of the globe. My vanilla Kansas childhood in no way armed me with the cultural knowledge and worldly experience that I needed to embrace this project.

Thanks to vast archives, news agency coverage and military photographs, as well as personal input from a slew of Vietnam veterans combined with courteous information from a host of Vietnamese immigrants, I was able to maintain the integrity of the meticulous research necessary for a book of this scope.

The process itself was painful. For both of us. Tammy, obviously, because she bared her soul to expose the most delicate, private parts of herself as she scraped back the scars of her past, unmasking nearly-forgotten scenes and events (some so horrific that she'd suppressed them for a lifetime) in order to winnow those that would illuminate her roots, interpret her motives, clarify her decisions and broaden her story. Me, because—quite frankly—there's no room for timidity and barely any allowance for tact when questioning, quizzing, even cross-examining someone to unearth the life-altering events, pivotal moments, subconscious choices, unrecognized influence and non-verbalized uncertainties (along with the persistent hopes and dreams) that shaped her character and formed her future.

In the end, I believe the growth was well worth the effort, the final product definitely worth the endless probing. And I'll be forever grateful for both the experience and the bond I share with this resilient, phenomenal woman. A woman I've come to love like a sister.

About Tammy

Tammy (Thuận) Fadler is the President/ CEO of Commercial International Properties and Signature Properties, whose consistent production ranks them in the top 1% of the real estate industry. Recipient of numerous professional and community awards, Tammy is a Star Power "Star" Speaker as well as a Vistage International Approved Speaker. She teaches workshops on courage, on following your dream and on discovering your passion and purpose. Armed with her *If you can believe it, you can achieve it!* motto, she motivates and inspires audiences at both personal and business levels throughout the U.S. and internationally. Mother of two and grandmother of five, she enjoys gardening, world travel and competitive ballroom dance.

To learn more about her workshops and speaking availability, visit her online at www.tammyfadler.com. To learn more about her real estate business, visit www.talktotammy.com.

About Carol

Carol McAdoo Rehme fell in love with words at the age of two, with writing at age eight. She earned a degree in journalism from Wichita State University and, after a lengthy stint as a professional storyteller, chose to meld her love of oral tales with the written word. She is the award-winning author of *Chicken Soup for the Soul: Book of Christmas Virtues, Chicken Soup for the Soul: Empty Nesters, The Ultimate Christmas* and multiple gift books. Nestled at the foothills of Colorado's Front Range, Carol writes and edits from a historic Victorian home she shares with her husband Norman. Both of them thrive on frequent visits from their four children and nine grandchildren. Visit her online at www.rehme.com.

Acknowledgements

Stunned by what they knew of her, Tammy's friends and audiences have pleaded for more of her stories. They wanted to understand where she came from, how she survived and how she arrived. They are the sole reason this book exists.

As a team, we clambered through the world of rediscovery, rehashing and refinement. Tammy's courage and honesty put us on the path to create this book as an inspiration to others to dream. To overcome obstacles. To persevere.

Khánh Hội is an ever-present reminder that it takes a village to raise a book. And to those villagers, we offer our sincere gratitude:

TAMMY's life coaches, Dr. Fred Grosse and Victoria Sinclair and the Tall Poppies for opening her soul to the possibility of a fulfilling life, one lived with passion and purpose.

Howard and Barbara Brinton and the Star Power family who continue to support Tammy through her journey, challenging her to reset her glass ceiling and find the blue sky above.

Tom and Betty Hill, Mickey and Terri Olsen and the Eagles for friendship and guidance. They point her toward new horizons, constantly raising the bar of success.

Rella Hawkins, for guidance and wisdom through "A Course in Miracles" and the discovery of unconditional love.

Tuesday Sisters Gail French, Glenda Williamson, Pat Sherman and Nick French (the *best* Token Male ever) for their deepest friendship, encouragement and unwavering support.

Dick Fadler and the Fadler Family for friendship, inclusion and full acceptance.

John and "Mom Shirley" Elliott and the Elliott clan for substituting as family when Tammy needed them most.

Ba, Má and Tammy's brothers and sisters, without whom the book simply wouldn't exist.

Tammy's children and grandchildren—Ginny, Cory, Rich, Sheri, Clayton, R. J., Russell, Courtney and Caitlyn—for love and sustenance through her long hours of work. They are her rocks; they keep her going.

Her staff and agents at Signature Properties for their abiding faith in Tammy.

Brian Jud and his dedicated team for publishing and marketing expertise.

Marsha Shepley, Don Peterson, Sally Borgerson and Rita Kayser for their input and proofreading during the creation of this book.

Tracey Smart for her dedication and valuable support throughout both the process and the journey during the past eighteen years.

✦ ✦ ✦

CAROL's husband Norman for assisting, believing, encouraging . . . and enduring. It would have been a lonely and painful journey without him.

Dear friends Vickie Elliott and Jean Richert for championing her through times of writer's feast and writer's famine.

Carita Barlow, Pam Goldstein and Carol Richey for critical eyes and valuable input.

Donna Cooner Gines for instigating isolated retreats at the Abbey of St. Walburga, a slice of heaven, but sometimes writer's hell.

Carol's long-time writing group—Jean Bell, Helen Colella, Lynn Dean, Sally Engeman, Kerrie Flanagan, Ellen Javernick, Maryjo Faith Morgan, Linda Osmundson, Peter Springberg and LeAnn Thieman for urging, purging and prodding.

Tammy's nephew Nguyễn Thanh Hùng (Bi) for tediously translating and correcting Carol's primitive Vietnamese.

Miss Edna Wheatley, Carol's high school English teacher, for wielding a wicked red pencil and expecting high standards so many decades ago.

Our early readers: Carita, Doug and Diane, Eric, Gail, Glenda, Kayla, Norm, Pam, Pat, Phyllis, Tom and Betty, Tracy,

Vic and Wayne for questioning the process and influencing the outcome.

✦ ✦ ✦

And, of course, sincerest appreciation for Má—whose pragmatic outlook inspired us to roll up our sleeves, clench our teeth and "Just do!"